THE COM
COFFEE COOKBOOK

MW01130165

From Beginner to Home-Barista | 365 Days of Delicious Coffee Recipes for Preparing the Perfect Brew in the Comfort of your Home

By

Jordan Lancaster

TABLE OF CONTENTS

INTRODUCTION

The world of coffee has seen immense growth in recent years and it's no wonder why; coffee is an amazingly complex beverage that can be enjoyed in a multitude of ways. It's always good to know more about what you're drinking or roasting and this book will expand the minds of coffee enthusiasts everywhere. Learn everything about making delicious coffee recipes and enjoy delicious recipes for the ultimate coffee experience.

Coffee is the most well-known and popular beverage in the world and is loved by people of all ages. The first reference to coffee is in an Arab version of the bible, where it's called qahwa. Coffee was also mentioned as a medicinal drink by Chinese Arab traders who referred to it as kahweh or qahwah. This rich history may be surprising considering coffee's controversy within religious circles and its less than desirable reputation today due to its toxic ingredients.

In the Middle East, where coffee originated, the beverage is taken very seriously and is not only offered to guests but expected. While most American coffee drinkers can barely tolerate their morning caffeinated cup of espresso, many Middle Eastern cultures consider a meal without a cup of coffee to be unacceptable. Moreover, in some other countries it is forbidden to eat or drink anything other than water from sunrise until the actual sunset during the month of Ramadan. During this time participants abstain from food, water, smoking and sexual activity during daylight hours and are limited in their intake of fluids after nightfall. Coffee drinking may decrease hunger pains that come with fasting because caffeine increases your metabolism and suppresses appetite.

Middle East coffee culture is not limited to adults. As with any other part of the world where coffee is taken seriously, it makes its way into the lives of children. Many families in Arab countries begin a child's day with a cup for breakfast. There are also various types of flavored coffee beverages that are offered in restaurants specifically aimed at children.

Arabic coffee is made from boiling finely ground coffee beans in water, resulting in a thick, syrupy beverage called "sahlep" or "qahweh." The sugar and spices used to flavor Arabic coffee vary according to region and personal taste, but many people prefer this coffee very sweet with no spices at all. In Syria, the sugar content is less than one gram per cup.

Choosing coffee beans may sometimes be a difficult process due to the wide variety of coffee varieties and bean mixes available from across the world. The globe is supplied with coffee beans in sizes varying from over sixty known kinds of coffee plants by more than forty-five coffee exporting nations, all of which utilize distinct classification systems. It makes sense that coffee would require a confusing java lingo! Fortunately, there are straightforward categories that may be used to group coffee terminology from the mountain to the market.

An aromatic scent wafts through the house and attracts you to the original source: the coffee. Regardless of whether the coffee beans are roasted, ground or simply prepared, it is always an extraordinary experience. But how did it come about, how did this thirst for coffee, which can be observed around the world, develop? From its origins in the highlands of Ethiopia through the Ottoman Empire to your kitchen, the coffee plant and its beans have already left a long way behind.

In addition, not all coffee is actually created equal. Some varieties taste mild, others fruity, and each country inspires with its own flavor notes that unfold. Depending on how you love your coffee, coffee beans from certain growing areas are best for you. From the growing area to the harvest, to roasting, grinding and preparation, there are many secrets with coffee that decide whether it is enjoyment or annoyance. From the unknown shrub to one of the most important commercial goods in the world - a lot has happened here in a few hundred years. Facts about the different types of coffee, from Arabica to Robusta, are just as interesting as further details about cultivation, special features of the coffee plant and the working conditions of the coffee farmers.

Would you have thought that coffee was discovered by goats and that the coffee beans are actually coffee cherries? In its history, coffee was also banned from time to time, sometimes cursed and sometimes idolized. It never got boring and the triumphant advance around the world cannot be stopped. Nevertheless, there are lovers and opponents of coffee - and countless forms of preparation, myths and peculiarities about the aromatic beans.

It's not just the discovery and the cultivation itself that are worth another look. Discover for yourself the special features that have to be taken into account during preparation and learn more about the differences in preparation in individual countries. Because from espresso in Italy to mocha in Turkey, there are countless variations that are guaranteed to bring variety to your table.

Come along on a voyage of discovery about coffee and get to know the most popular recipes from all over the world! You will actually be surprised by the variety of preparation options as well as the special features of the coffee plants!

CHAPTER 1:
The Harvesting of Beans

Even if you usually go to a coffee shop for your daily cup, you could theoretically do most aspects of coffee preparation yourself at home, whether that's brewing, making your own blends, or even roasting your own green beans. The recent spike in interest in single-origin and other artesian coffees means this is even easier to achieve than it was a few years ago. Even relatively small towns often have at least one coffee shop that focuses on high-quality, single-origin beans, and you can purchase small batches of green beans—and the supplies you need to roast them—very easily online.

Coffee plants are notoriously finicky; a slight change in the elevation, rainfall, or average temperature in the growing region can have a profound effect on the ultimate taste of the beverage in your cup. Even if you could get a coffee tree to grow in a temperate region like Europe or the United States, the payoff would be a long time coming; while a coffee tree can produce beans for several years in healthy conditions, it doesn't usually start to produce its best-tasting beans until it's around 5 years old.

Even though you probably won't be able to start your own coffee nursery at home, learning about the journey a bean takes from the time it's planted until it ends up at the roaster can give you some excellent insights into why certain coffee tastes the way it does, and can help you to make more educated guesses about the flavor notes of a certain cultivar or growing region when you're buying unfamiliar beans, especially if you like to shop online and won't have anyone around that you can ask about the cup profile.

There are a lot of different factors that determine the quality level of the end cup. The genetic make-up of the plant will give it a certain starting quality and flavor potential, which will then be influenced by the environmental conditions during the flowering and fruit production stages of the bean's development, as well as by the farming practices in place and how the bean is processed and stored post-harvest. At each of these stages in the bean's life, the quality potential has to be carefully preserved to give you a good-tasting final cup.

The information that follows in this book will walk you through the life of a coffee bean, from the first moment the plant begins to grow until it's dried at the mill and ready to be shipped to the roaster. By the time you really reach the end of this book, you'll have a much deeper understanding of exactly what has to happen to bring you your morning joe—and how farmers make sure the taste is exactly what you're looking for.

Within the arabica family, there are dozens of what are called cultivars, or cultivated varieties, which you can actually think of as being similar to the varietals of wine grapes. The same cultivar could still taste drastically different depending on the growing conditions, but which cultivar the beans are grown from determines what range of flavors is possible.

The elevation at which the coffee tree is grown is arguably the most important factor in the developing the taste of the bean. Arabica coffees can grow at a wide range of elevations, from around 1,800 feet to around 6,300 feet above sea level; generally speaking, the higher-grown the coffee, the better the quality. The climate tends to be cooler in higher elevations; combined with the lower oxygen levels in the air, this makes the coffee trees grow more slowly at higher elevations, resulting in a smaller, denser bean (sometimes called "hard beans").

A coffee grown at a higher altitude is likely to be more acidic and aromatic, with more complexity in the cup. Coffee grown at lower elevations will be flatter overall, with less acidity and fewer flavor notes, making them good as a background presence in a blend. The fact that these beans grow more slowly also means that the yield per plant tends to be lower, which perhaps even more than the improved flavor tends to make them more expensive.

As a general rule of thumb, coffees grown at certain elevations will have certain specific flavor notes. Those grown at a very low elevation (2,500 feet above sea level or lower) tend to have a somewhat bland taste that may have earthy notes. Those grown at a low elevation (2,500-3,000 feet) are a bit more complex but still have a subtle, mild flavor. Medium-grown coffees (3,000-4,000 feet) tend to taste sweet and have a relatively low acidity. High-grown coffees (4,000-5,000 feet) have a slightly higher acidity that may give them a sweet citrus taste, though they often also have sweet vanilla notes or deep nutty tones, resulting in an often complex final cup. The most prized coffees, those grown at very high elevations (5,000 feet and higher) tend to have the highest acidity and can give you notes ranging from fruity to floral to spicy or wine-like, depending on what's done to the bean after it's picked.

While low-grown coffee is often seen as lower-quality, there are always exceptions to every rule. Coffee from the Kona district of Hawaii, for example, can't be grown at elevations over 2,000 feet; the island is far enough north of the equator that the climate is too cold at higher altitudes. Kona coffee is prized for its soft sweetness and low acidity, but the low density of the beans means it has to be handled carefully and can easily be ruined through over-roasting.

While the climate often goes hand in hand with the elevation, it also has its own influences on the taste of the bean. Especially important is whether the coffee is grown in shade or direct sunlight. In warmer regions, coffee plants can burn if exposed to too much direct sunlight, giving the beans a bitter aftertaste and flatter overall profile. Shade-grown coffee develops more slowly, giving it more complexity. The climate also affects the length of the growing season and at what point in the year the fruit is at its ideal ripeness. Even minor changes in temperature and rainfall levels can have a big impact on the quality of the beans.

The contents and quality of the soil also affect the bean. Not only will the correct ratio of minerals and nutrients encourage healthy growth of the plant but the minerals absorbed through the root will affect which oils and compounds are most prominent in the fruit and seeds. The same cultivar grown at the same elevation would taste very different if grown in an acidic soil, like one based on volcanic rock, than it would if grown in a more basic soil of limestone or clay.

These natural variations in climate, altitude and soil contents are also affected by the techniques the farmer uses to grow his plants. Farms in Central and South America are likely to prune their trees more regularly and use systems of irrigation and fertilization to encourage growth. Indonesian farms don't tend to prune their trees as regularly, and in certain regions of Africa, coffee beans are still harvested from wild-grown trees that undergo no cultivation at all. The more cultivation is employed, the more consistent the beans from that farm will generally be.

How much of this information you have about a particular bean will likely depend on where you shop. A coffee shop that roasts in-house is likely to at least be able to at least tell you which farm the beans came from, including its elevation and typical climate, as well as the bean's cultivar. As you get more familiar with different popular regions, you'll likely start to see patterns and trends in the taste profiles of beans from these areas.

Harvest Your Beans

From the point in time when the coffee plants bloom to the harvest of the ripe coffee cherries, it takes a lot of time, depending on the altitude. It can therefore take nine months before the farmers can pick the cherries so that they are actually ripe and of convincing quality. At higher altitudes in the mountains it takes longer before a harvest is possible than at lower ones. If there are up to two harvests a year at lower altitudes, this is not necessarily common for highland coffee, which is referred to as such from a height of around 1,000 meters.

It takes about three years before the crops can be used. According to previous experience, the maximum productivity of the coffee plants is achieved after about six to eight years. Afterwards, productivity slowly decreases. It should also be noted that the harvest times vary from region to region. The coffee harvest itself takes about ten to twelve weeks. It is actually very important that you do not wait long to harvest once the coffee cherries are ripe. Because it only takes around two weeks for ripe cherries to become overripe and no longer usable coffee cherries.

As soon as the coffee cherries are ripe, they have to be harvested. There are normally three different methods that are used and are common for this.

1. Picking

The most complex method of picking the ripe cherries is picking. With this method, ripe coffee cherries are picked individually by hand. The specialty is that only ripe cherries are harvested and the rest can ripen until they are also ready to be harvested. With this method, a pre-selection takes place and all coffee cherries of the bushes are given the opportunity to reach the optimal degree of ripeness. This makes picking very expensive and time-consuming, but it significantly increases the quality of the harvest.

2. Hand stripping

When stripping by hand, a special comb is used to pick the coffee cherries. The workers use their combs to harvest all the coffee cherries on a bush at once, including those that are overripe and those that are still unripe. Only then are the coffee cherries sorted so that stripping takes less time. The costs are also lower. However, with this method, the coffee cherries that are not yet or no longer suitable for further processing are also harvested.

3. Machine stripping

The fastest and easiest method for humans is machine stripping. This is a mechanical form of harvest, in which all the coffee cherries are harvested at once with one machine. This is the method in which a lot of sorting has to be done afterwards, since in addition to coffee cherries, leaves and stones also end up in the harvest. The use of machine stripping takes the strain off people during the harvest, but leads to a lower quality and removes coffee cherries that might not have been ripe for a few days or weeks.

After the successful harvest, further steps for processing the coffee beans can be initiated. Harvesting at the right time is actually extremely important for all subsequent steps and, at least when picking, requires the coffee farmers' expertise and a keen eye. For the harvest, more and more coffee plantation owners and many small farmers are joining forces to form cooperatives. Higher prices for the coffee on sale, as well as bonuses for working with Fairtrade and other organizations, make things a little easier for coffee farmers when it comes to prices received and quality of life.

After the harvest, the coffee cherries are further processed, weighed and exported or processed on site in roasting plants. There are regional differences in the approach. The decisive factor on the world market is the weight of the green coffee, not the weight of the entire coffee cherries, which is of course higher than that of the processed coffee cherries.

Once the coffee beans are grinded into their powdered form, their surface area increases exponentially, and so does the rate at which they spoil. Hence, the best course of action is to store the coffee beans in their whole form, and grind instantly before you make a drink.

If you like to buy ground coffee from the market, make sure the containers are airtight. Once you open these airtight containers, it is best to consume the contents of the container within two weeks. Hence, it is best to buy pre-ground coffee in small batches.

CHAPTER 2:
Processing and Roasting the Coffee Beans

Bring out the Beans!

Roasting is an important step in developing the flavors of the coffee bean. Truly anyone can be a home roaster, but even if that's not your plan, understanding the ways in which roasting impacts the flavor of the beans will help you to be a better-informed consumer of the beverage.

Roasting Coffee Beans

One of the last steps before preparation is further processing after the coffee beans have been harvested. Because the coffee beans are not simply picked and then brewed. Rather, it is necessary to roast the beans beforehand and grind them in the next step.

Only then are the previously harvested beans ready for you to enjoy a coffee. Caution should be exercised during this processing step, as a lot can be done wrong with roasting. The wrong roasting results in a bitter taste and thus spoils the coffee very quickly.

After the harvest and before roasting, the first thing to do is to process the coffee cherries. Various methods are available for this. A distinction is actually made between dry, semi-dry and wet processing, which we will take a closer look at at this point:

The dry preparation

Usually, the stripping method continues with the dry processing of the coffee cherries. To do this, spread the coffee cherries of the same size together on a surface to dry. It takes around three to five weeks, if the coffee cherries are turned several times, until the kernels, i.e. the beans, rattle when shaken. Then the coffee cherries are sufficiently dry that the pulp and parchment skin around the beans can be removed. The beans stay in what is known as the silver skin and after this processing they are packed in large bags.

The semi-dry preparation

A middle way between dry and wet processing is semi-dry processing, which requires less water than is the case with wet processing. After harvesting, the coffee cherries are freed from the pulp in a water basin or in a flood channel, just like in wet processing. They are then dried immediately and without fermentation. The parchment skin is then peeled, then sorted again and, in the next step, the resulting green coffee is filled into sacks.

The wet treatment

This form of processing is reserved for the particularly high-quality coffee cherries that have been picked individually by hand. This method requires a lot of water and is less suitable for very large crops. With this form of processing, the coffee cherries are pre-sorted in a water basin or in a flood channel a maximum of 24 hours after harvest. The pulp is then removed by machine, in which case pieces of the pulp still remain on the beans, as the parchment skin is not removed. In contrast to dry processing!

Now the beans obtained in this way remain in a large fermentation tank for a day or two so that fermentation takes place. During this fermentation, the remaining pulp of the beans loosens. Only after this fermentation process has ended do the workers wash the beans, dry them in the sun, on drying tables made of fine-mesh wire netting or in a few hours in a machine and then remove the parchment skin. The silver skin is removed as far as possible, although it cannot always be removed. The fermentation and drying, ideally in the sun, results in a very high quality of these beans. Finally, the beans are sorted again before filling.

For all types of preparation, it is necessary that the coffee cherries are sorted before this step. This intermediate step is only important for stripping, because when picking, sorting by hand is no longer necessary right from the start. Unripe or overripe coffee cherries are sorted out as well as possible. Branches, twigs or stones that get into the container of the harvested coffee cherries during mechanical stripping must also be sorted out here. For the highest possible quality, the harvest is therefore sorted before processing begins.

After the successful preparation, the coffee beans can be roasted. After roasting, the coffee is almost ready to be brewed and then drunk. It is not for nothing that we are talking about elaborate production, since there is actually a lot of work behind every pound of coffee that you can buy.

Roasting is very important for coffee, as this is where the beans develop their typical brown color, aroma and acidity. Coffee beans are always roasted before they are ground in the next step. The weight of the beans changes during roasting, as does the smell and size. In fact, the temperature and roasting time can produce different flavors from two same types of coffee beans. Incorrect roasting also spoils the beans, which then develop a bitter taste. So it is not a matter of special varieties, but a special process that is used during roasting. Knowing the perfect temperature and the optimal roasting time is therefore very important here.

When roasting, a distinction is made between hot air and drum roasting in order to achieve the desired result:

Roasting in the hot air process

In this case, the coffee beans are roasted at high temperatures of up to 600 degrees. Since such high temperatures are used here, roasting only takes place for a short time, i.e. for two to a maximum of five minutes. After roasting, the beans can be cooled with either water or air and later packaged.

Advantages of the procedure:

Very large quantities of green coffee are processed in a short time. It is the fastest form of roasting.

Disadvantages of the procedure:

Unfortunately, the high temperatures and the short duration lead to inconsistent results. It can even happen that the beans are still raw inside, which is undesirable.

The drum roast

For smaller quantities of green coffee, drum roasting is recommended, which is carried out at a lower temperature of 200 degrees for 14 to 25 minutes. The longer period of time leads to gentler results when roasting, which allows aromas and acids to develop optimally. After roasting, the beans are also cooled and packaged here.

Advantages of the procedure:

Beans are roasted gently and evenly. Flavors and acids develop perfectly and even acids that are not good for the stomach can be broken down.

Disadvantages of the procedure:

This process is unsuitable for large quantities of green coffee. The beans take longer to roast, and drum roasting takes a long time if you use multiple passes for large quantities of green coffee. It also takes a lot of expertise to finish roasting at the right moment. If the roast is too long or too short, no convincing result is to be expected. You may have heard of different degrees of roast that play a role in coffee. Robusta beans take longer to roast than Arabica beans. Basically, however, the degree of roasting of the coffee beans determines a lot more than just the color of the beans. The aroma is also largely influenced by the degree of roasting. The following degrees of roasting are common:

- light roast (cinnamon roast)
- medium roast (American roast)
- strong roast (Viennese roast)
- double roast (French roast)
- Italian roasting (espresso roasting)
- Spanish roasting (Torrefacto roasting)

In many cases, the roasted beans are mixed before the coffee is ground. The term "blend" is used here, as the coffee blends are called. Of course, there is also coffee that is single-origin or comes from a single cultivation country. The term "terroir" refers to beans from a coffee region to which no other beans have been added. In the case of beans labeled "Pure Origin", the coffee comes from a single country, but from several regions. Such a mixture is often a little more balanced in terms of taste and aroma than is the case with "Terroir". However, there are often coffee blends that have "100 percent Arabica" on the packaging, but this does not mean that the beans cannot come from different countries. For example, there could actually be a mixture of coffee beans from Brazil and Colombia or from Guatemala and Honduras.

Last but not least, there are coffee blends in which the Robusta and Arabica varieties are mixed. The coffee beans are not mixed before roasting, but only in the next step before packing.

Perhaps you are now wondering what are the reasons for such mixtures, i.e. for blends. Coffee beans are mixed after roasting for the following reasons:

- Maintaining the taste
- Cost reasons
- Achieving balanced mixtures

Sometimes the beans lack taste. In this case, a harmonious result is possible if the beans are mixed together and not only beans from one region are used. Knowing when it would be beneficial and when it would be a disadvantage to blend the coffee beans is essential. After all, each region has special features with regard to its coffee that must first be recognized so that coffee blends are ultimately convincing in terms of their taste and aroma. Last but not least, it is actually also cheaper to make blends instead of single-origin coffee. This is mainly due to the fact that beans with an inferior aroma are difficult to sort out. Rather, other beans literally outshine these weaker ones, so to speak, so that a harmonious end result is achieved - at least if the mixture is right. The next time you buy coffee, pay attention to the individual information on the packaging - it is interesting how often these details are otherwise overlooked.

The inside of the coffee bean undergoes chemical changes during the roasting process that drastically affect its flavor. The sugars in the bean are caramelized; acids that were buried deep inside the bean are brought to the surface. How many of these changes the bean is allowed to undergo will determine the ultimate taste profile.

Beans that aren't roasted are called "green." If you tried to brew green coffee beans, you'd get a beverage that's sharp and vegetal, with bitter undertones like an over-brewed green tea. The roasting process is instrumental to bringing out the flavors we associate with coffee.

The lightest drinkable roast level is a cinnamon roast, named for the color of the beans at this level, not because the taste will have any traces of cinnamon. These roasts will have the highest acidity and a relatively weak body. It will be more aromatic and complex than the same bean at a cinnamon roast; the majority of beans need to be roasted at least to this level.

The next darkest is the medium or "American roast," so-named because of its popularity in North America. This is the level at which many beans are at their peak complexity, where the flavor oils have been fully extracted but the acids haven't burned off too much.

Finally, there are the dark roasts. The border between medium and dark roasts can be loosely drawn at the point where more than half the acids of the bean have burned off, replaced by a pungent, dark flavor and a fuller body. The lightest is called a full roast or Vienna roast and it is the level at which many beans are at their most aromatic. Next is the French roast, which is also called espresso roast because this is the level at which many beans are best-suited to that brewing method. The darkest roast is the Italian roast. It is the least acidic with the thickest body but with less complexity and aroma.

There are some beans that will taste good at a variety of roast levels, while others are more finicky and best-suited to a particular style. Beyond the accepted standards of the industry, roast level is in many ways a personal preference. Those who grew up drinking American-style coffee may find darker roast levels too pungent or bitter, while those accustomed to espresso would find a light roast thin and weak. Determining which roast level you prefer can help you choose your coffees as you're working on your ideal blend.

CHAPTER 3:
The Different Types of Coffee

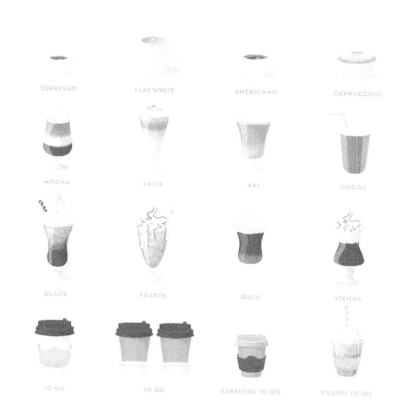

Basically, a distinction is made between the two types of coffee Arabica and Robusta. Like all coffee plants, both varieties belong to the red family. There are about 124 other varieties in the world, but their importance is rather minor. That is why the Arabica and Robusta varieties are normally always referred to when it comes to the differences and similarities between the most important types of coffee. At this point you will learn what is hidden behind these names and how they differ from each other in the first place.

The "Coffea arabica" variety is cultivated particularly frequently - in fact, around three times as often in the world as is the case with "Coffea canephora" (Robusta). The share of Coffea arabica is around 70 percent and that of Robusta is 30 percent. Arabica is particularly popular in Latin America. The Robusta coffee plants are actually mainly found in Indonesia, India and Vietnam.

The plants, or rather bushes, look similar up close in terms of leaves, the color of the flowers and the coffee cherries. From a distance, however, there are many differences, as the Arabica plants are around six to eight meters high and the Robusta plants can reach heights of up to ten meters, so that a difference in height can be seen in adult coffee plants.

If there are only a few really visible differences at first, the beans of the two types of coffee can be clearly distinguished from one another. Because the beans of the Robusta plants are smaller and rounder and the Arabica beans are flatter, slightly larger and have an S-shaped incision on the surface. The Robusta beans, on the other hand, have a straight cut.

In fact, in addition to the looks, there are actually quite big differences between the two types of coffee. It starts with the caffeine content, as Arabica beans only have 1.1 to 1.7 percent caffeine. Robusta beans, on the other hand, have a caffeine content of 2 to 4.5 percent and are generally rated somewhat lower in quality than Arabica beans. Arabica coffee is often less bitter and more aromatic in terms of taste. But that doesn't necessarily have to actually be the case, as there are excellent Robusta beans that taste very mild and aromatic. Arabica beans can also taste bitter, as many factors ultimately influence the taste, as you already know.

It is interesting that, especially with an espresso, both types are often combined for a perfect taste result. So it's worth trying a little, paying attention to the quality and not categorically excluding the Robusta beans. After all, there are good reasons why both varieties continue to be grown worldwide - albeit with different weights in terms of quantity.

When it comes to growing, there are significant differences between the two popular strains, so the robusta plant actually bears its name for good reason. The plants are more resilient and can even cope with occasional night frosts or warmer temperatures. With regard to the altitude, the plants are also more resistant than Arabica plants and even parasites and pests cannot destroy the robust coffee plants as quickly. Arabica plants are more sensitive and to make matters worse, they are also affected by special pests at altitudes below 900 meters. The higher elevations, which are necessary for their cultivation, slow down the growth and lead to less frequent harvests. These peculiarities and the greater sensitivity of the plants themselves mean that the price for these beans on the world market is automatically higher than for Robusta beans.

A portrait of the arabica plant:

- dominates the world market
- The ripening time of the beans 4-5 days
- grows best at altitudes between 900 and 2,000 meters
- Needs an average of 15 to 24 degrees to grow
- their bean has an S-shaped slot

The Robusta plant in portrait:

- particularly robust and resistant
- grows from a height of 400 meters
- can even withstand temperatures of up to 30 degrees
- their beans have a higher caffeine content (up to 4 percent)
- Because of the high caffeine content, pests stay away
- their bean has a straight slot
- their beans are smaller than the arabica beans

In fact, Robusta coffee has gotten a pretty bad reputation, but it's in no way always justified. Coffee lovers these days often only want coffee that is made from 100 percent Arabica beans. This is not least due to the lower price of the Robusta beans, which together with the imprint "100 percent Robusta" ensure that the beans have a cheap aftertaste for many. In addition, it often happens that Robusta beans are roasted incorrectly, making them particularly bitter and inedible for many palates. The beans have to be roasted longer and therefore darker than is the case with Arabica beans. Please note, for example, that a real espresso cannot be perfect without a Robusta component. This is why it makes so much sense to deal with roasting coffee as well as grinding it. The best and highest quality beans are of little use if they are processed incorrectly.

Flavor of Coffees

Some coffees have flavor notes that are more pronounced than others; some natural processed Kenyans and Ethiopians, for example, can have intense berry flavors, while some coffees from Mexico can taste powerfully of cocoa. Generally, though, the notes in coffee are more subtle. Most blends are designed more with an eye to the overall taste profile of the cup than they are to bringing out a specific flavor. If you actually want a coffee that actually tastes like vanilla or hazelnut, you'll need to add more than just different kinds of coffee beans into the mix.

You'll find a lot of different flavor options in the coffee aisle of the supermarket. Most of these commercial coffees get their extra flavor from a mixture of chemicals, which is adhered to the beans using a syrup or other binding agent. These residues can be left behind in your grinder and coffee maker, affecting the flavor of your other coffee for weeks afterward. What's more, manufacturers will often use their flavored coffee offerings as a way to get rid of their lower-quality beans, since the taste of this artificial flavoring is so strong it completely obscures all but the most powerful notes in the coffee. By adding your own flavorings, you actually can make sure you're only using natural ingredients and quality coffee beans. You also get to control the balance of the coffee to the added flavors, allowing the natural notes of the beans to shine through.

Coffee beans are naturally porous, absorbing flavors that are nearby. This can really be a very bad thing if you're storing your coffee beans in the freezer but is great when you're trying to flavor your beans, as they'll naturally pick up the flavors of anything you seal in with them.

There are a few different ingredients you can use to flavor your coffee, some of which can be utilized in a variety of ways for a different level and type of flavor. While none of these will linger in your grinder and coffee maker nearly as long as artificial flavorings, you may want to clean your equipment between flavors, especially if you're using extracts, nuts, or other ingredients that can leave oils behind.

If you use a burr grinder for your coffee beans, make sure to remove any extra spices, fruits, or nuts you've added to your beans, as they can damage or jam the burrs. You may even want to buy a small blade grinder to use with your flavored mixes. These can usually handle hard-shelled add-ins (and even if they are damaged, are much cheaper to replace) and they're easier to clean when it's time to switch to a new flavor.

- **Extracts**

You'll find two kinds of extracts in the baking aisle: real and imitation. Real extracts are made by soaking mashed up ingredients like vanilla pods or cinnamon sticks in a liquid (usually some kind of alcohol) while imitation extracts are made by combining chemicals together that simulate the flavors. When you're using them to flavor coffee, you want to use real extract; imitation flavors are more likely to degrade over time and can have a bitter aftertaste.

Popular extract options that work well with coffee are vanilla, peppermint, cinnamon, coconut, orange, and maple. Use 3-4 tablespoons of extra for a pound of coffee. You'll probably find it easier to dump the beans into a large mixing bowl, tossing in the flavoring, and then pouring it back in the canister, rather than trying to add the extract right into the container.

- **Whole spices**

Spices like cinnamon, cardamom, clove, and ginger pair well with the taste of coffee and can be used to add a bit of extra flavor to your beans. You'll get the most flavor if you crush the spices before putting them into the blend, especially with hard-shelled options like anise and nutmeg. Add about ¼ cup of crushed, whole spices for each pound of coffee beans and allow the flavors to mingle for 3-4 days before brewing.

- **Ground spices**

Ground spices will have a very similar effect on the flavor to whole spices, but they'll need to be utilized a little differently. Rather than pour them in with the beans, you can mix ground spices in with your coffee after it is ground, just before you pour it into the brew basket. This can make it the perfect option for people who want to use a burr grinder but don't want to have to worry about picking the flavoring agents out of their beans. Add about 1/8 teaspoon of spice for every 2 tablespoons of coffee (about the amount you'll use for one serving).

The flavors listed in the "whole spices" section above are equally good options in their ground forms, but you also have other choices when you go this route. Pre-made mixes like pumpkin pie or apple pie spice complement the taste of coffee well, or you could use ground cocoa to enhance the coffee's chocolatey notes. Chicory is a root that's often ground up and added to coffee in France and French-settled regions like New

Orleans. Originally used to stretch coffee supplies during lean times, it has a taste similar to coffee but adds a spiciness that pairs especially well with darker roasts.

- **Nuts**

The oils in the nuts are going to impact the flavor of the coffee beans more than the aromatics. Because of this, you'll get the most extra flavor by crushing the nuts first to release those oils, and then tossing them in with the beans. Add about a tablespoon of crushed nuts for every cup of beans to start, and adjust from there to give you the intensity of flavor you're looking for.

- **Fruit**

Fresh fruit has a lot of moisture, which can contribute to the growth of mold in your coffee beans if they're stored together. This leaves you two options if you want to add fruity flavor to your coffee: dried fruit or citrus rinds. Dried berries, cherries, or apricots can bring out the natural fruitiness of light-roasted coffee, though their flavor may be too subtle to be effective with fuller-bodied blends. Citrus peel, on the other hand, can be a great way to brighten up a darker roast. As with nuts, you should start with about a tablespoon for each cup of beans.

It can give you everything from the bright acidity of citrus to the lingering bitterness of dark chocolate—sometimes in a single cup. Honing your palate and creating artful blends are both skills that you have to learn, and like any skill, they take practice to fully develop. Experiment with as many different kinds of coffee as you can and keep track of which ones you like and which you don't. Even as you hone in on which regions and roast levels tend to be most to your liking, go outside your comfort zone every once in a while; you just might find something that surprises you.

Most coffee shops that sell their beans in bulk will let you buy in any quantity. If you're getting a few different kinds to try out, a quarter pound should be enough to brew a few cups and get an overall sense of the coffee, and you won't run the risk of the beans going stale before you use them. Most coffees are at their peak flavor 7-10 days after roasting, so you don't want to let them sit around for too long.

Home-made coffee blends can also make great gifts, especially if you add flavoring. You can use extracts, spices, nuts, and fruits in combination to create your own recipes and make your blends truly unique. Remember that balance is the key. A more mellow coffee will be a better canvas for a lot of bold added flavors than one that already has a lot of depth and complexity.

Coffee is notoriously finicky, both as a plant and as a beverage. Slight changes in the growing conditions or roast times can have a big impact on the taste of the bean, and there will always be variations from batch to batch. Don't get frustrated if your blends don't turn out quite the way you expected, and be creative with your flavor combinations. With enough practice and experimentation, you can blend your way to the perfect cup.

Coffee Cost

There are several factors that affect coffee prices. Some countries, such as Iran, charge a higher price for coffee than others. However, many roasters sell their coffee for lower prices. The average consumer spends $13 at a coffee shop. You can also check out the average cost of a pound of coffee.

Average price of a cup of coffee in Iran

According to a recent Statista report, the average price of a cup of coffee in Iran is $0.46. In Iran, coffee is not the most popular beverage, and many people prefer tea. Although coffee is inexpensive in Iran, it's not cheap elsewhere. South Korea, for instance, charges an average of $7.77 for a cup of coffee. In the United States, the average cost of a cup of coffee is $3.77. Iran is among the cheapest countries to purchase coffee, with a cost of $0.46.

The Middle East has a diverse coffee culture, with five countries ranking among the world's most expensive. While tea is a staple beverage in much of Asia, coffee shops are becoming more common in countries like Iran. In the world, Luxembourg is the biggest consumer of coffee. By contrast, India, Pakistan, and Nepal drink the least coffee. In the Middle East, coffee consumption is growing rapidly. Moreover, coffee shops are opening in cities across the country, and there is an increased demand for specialty coffees.

Coffee is a popular beverage in the Middle East, and it's an integral part of hospitality. Middle Eastern coffee is dark, thick, and typically topped with spices like cardamom. Middle Eastern countries were some of the first to consume coffee. Today, it's almost as popular in the United Arab Emirates as in the U.S., but there are challenges associated with brewing coffee in these countries. Among these challenges is the poor quality of desalinized water, which makes it less suitable for brewing coffee. Additionally, cow's milk is thinner than normal, which increases the price of coffee.

Average price of a cup of coffee in Australia

In Australia, the average price of a cup of coffee is about $4.86, and that amount will probably only go up in the next few years. The price of coffee is driven by factors like global production, wages and incidental costs, such as the wholesale cost of caramel syrup. This is one of the reasons why coffee in Australia costs so much.

The latest reports have shown that the average price of a flat white is set to rise another 50 cents by the end of this year. This is the result of price hikes triggered by wild weather events and the volatility in the international bean market. In addition, rising cost of container shipments, transport, and other ingredients have contributed to the increase.

The coffee shops in Australia offer a variety of beverages, including tea and espresso drinks. Lattes are the most popular drinks and account for one third of all the coffee sold in the country. Flat whites are the second most popular beverages. Tea is the fourth most common beverage in Australia.

Average price of a cup of coffee in South Korea

Coffee is a staple drink in South Korea, and is relatively cheap there. A single cup can cost around W20,000 (about $14), which works out to roughly $0.10 per cup. Many cafes offer different types of coffee, and most list the price next to each. The most common type of coffee is the iced Americano. You can also find cheap, independent coffee shops across the country. Some of these are slightly more expensive than regular chains, while others are comparable in price.

Coffee prices vary based on the time of day and location. Most coffee shops offer discounted prices during off-peak hours. Starbucks, for instance, charges 4,100 won for a single cup of Americano. Other companies, such as McDonald's, are known for their cheap coffee.

According to SavingSpot, the average price of a cup of coffee in South Korean is $7.77. The countries with the highest average coffee prices include Kuwait, Qatar, and Switzerland. The reasons for the high prices are varied, including the foreign premium - South Koreans are used to paying more for imported goods. Other reasons for the high cost of coffee in South Korea include the high number of themed cafes, which tend to charge top dollar for their interactions.

Average price of a pound of coffee

Average price of a pound of coffee varies depending on the type and quality of coffee. Prices are also dependent on where you purchase the coffee. For example, specialty coffee shops may charge a higher price for coffee than you can find in a grocery store. You can also find inexpensive coffee for less than $10 per pound if you know where to look. But, the quality of coffee will cost you more. Prices may also fluctuate depending on the time of the year and the current coffee market.

According to the British Coffee Association, coffee is the most popular beverage in the world, with over 2 billion cups consumed every day. A recent polling survey by the National Coffee Association revealed that 66% of Americans drink coffee every day. Although coffee prices may seem expensive, many people still enjoy it.

The average price of a pound of coffee varies by country. A pound of coffee from Brazil can cost anywhere from $2.50 to $10, while coffee from Ethiopia can cost as much as $15 per pound. The price also varies by grade, with a higher grade costing anywhere from $6 to $15 per pound.

CHAPTER 4:
Equipment, Machinery and Tools

At the present time, coffee is a popular beverage worldwide. In fact, it is being sold cheaply in the form of 3-in-1 instant coffee mix sachets up to the most expensive ones that are sold in the coffee shop near you.

If you are so curious about how to make your favorite coffee at home, here's what you need to have:

Coffee Grinder

A coffee grinder is actually a device that is always used to grind whole coffee beans using blades (hence the name) to crack into a perfect size for coffee brewing. Some are manually operated while some are automatically operated (electric models).

- Manual Coffee Grinder
- Automatic Coffee Grinder

Coffee Maker

A coffee maker is actually an appliance or a kitchenware that is specifically designed to brew ground cocoa beans and whole coffee beans. It comes in different models; some are manual, some are automatic (fully electric models), some are built for a single purpose only (which consist of a single stove-top pot), some are made in brewing glassware, while some are built for multi-purpose brewing that is multi-functional (which means it can brew not just traditional coffee but can brew latte, espresso, and other coffee blends).

Coffee Filter

A coffee filter is a coffee-brewing kitchen utensil that serves as a strainer. Usually, it is made of disposable paper or the finest of wire mesh. It holds the coffee grounds so the water can pass through the contents and into the receiving coffee pot. The filter is shaped into a basket or cone to fit the different types of coffee makers.

Frother

A frother, also called a milk frother, is a handheld device that is specifically used to shake the liquids to an airy mixture of foam and bubbles. It is often used to whip hot and/or cold milk to thick foam that is added on top of coffee blends.

Coffee Mug

Last but not least, of course, you need your own coffee mug! Some coffee mugs come with a spoon, lid, mug cover/lid, and a coaster.

Types of Coffee Machines

There are several types of coffee machines, each with a different set of advantages and disadvantages. The higher-end models have more bells and whistles, such as espresso and milk frothing. They also take longer to brew, but offer more customization. Pour-overs and French presses, on the other hand, require more preparation and a more hands-on approach.

While the coffee making process may seem complicated, the basic parts of coffee machines include a heating element, reservoir, and coffee grounds. The heating element controls the temperature of water. A one-way valve in the heating tube and reservoir helps prevent overheating. A power cord supplies energy to the machine.

There are several types of coffee machines on the market, each with its own advantages and disadvantages. A low-end model might produce a decent cup of coffee, while a higher-end machine might produce a better-tasting cup of coffee. Pod coffee machines are great for people who need coffee in a hurry and don't want to spend time brewing coffee beans.

There are also built-in coffee machines, which are installed in cabinets or counters. They may require an external water reservoir and are fully plumbed. However, this type of machine may not be suitable for everyone as it's more expensive and requires a large room. It's also not suitable for occasional users.

Coffee machines also have several features that make them more user-friendly. For example, some models are made with milk frothing systems, so all you have to do is put a cup into the coffee machine and press a button. Besides making great coffee, these machines also help you save time by eliminating the need to manually tamp the coffee grounds.

Coffee machines are primarily divided into two types: drip machines and percolators. Each type has its own unique feature, but they have some similarities. Pod coffee machines are usually smaller than drip coffee machines, and their main function is to brew coffee. They usually use a paper filter. They produce a good cup of coffee that is full of flavor and aroma.

Coffee machines are a great investment for many households. There are many different models available, so you should choose the right one for your home. For example, you can choose a manual pour-over coffee maker for home use, or a cheaper model with an integrated grinder. You can get one that costs as low as 65 EUR.

If you're looking for a coffee machine with a built-in coffee pot, consider the Nespresso Vertuo Next. This machine offers Wi-Fi capabilities and an integrated ceramic burr grinder that ensures a perfect espresso. This machine also comes in six different colours, and is compatible with Bluetooth and WIFI.

Coffee makers usually have a heating element, which warms the water before it sprays it onto the coffee grounds. The heating element also helps to keep the coffee warm after it's brewed. A resistive heating element consists of a coiled wire, which heats when supplied with electricity. It is embedded in plaster or is set between an aluminum water tube and a metal warming plate underneath the coffee pot.

A semi-automatic espresso machine is another good option for home use. These machines are a replica of the machines found in cafes, but are less complex to operate. They are the ideal option for people who want to experiment with their espresso making skills. A semi-automatic machine will also let you control the amount of water in the espresso as well as the pressure and dosage.

If you want an instant brew, a single-serve coffee maker will do the job. It has a removable water reservoir and a digital display to set the amount of water to use. A special feature of these coffee machines is the "accubrew" setting, which weighs the coffee grounds as you add them to the basket. Moreover, this type of coffee maker is easy to clean and maintain.

Coffee enthusiasts may opt for a double-walled carafe coffee maker. This type of coffee maker has a stainless steel carafe that will keep your brew warm without overheating it. The machine also features a timer for brewing. It is a good choice for temporary living quarters. However, its durability may not be enough for everyday use.

If you want a freshly ground cup of coffee, you should buy a coffee maker with a built-in grinder. While this type of coffee maker is usually more expensive than models without a grinder, it can save you money and counter space. Standalone coffee grinders are often better at grinding coffee and can produce a variety of different brew styles. Some coffee drinkers swear that having a separate grinder makes a big difference in taste.

For a single-serve coffee drinker, pod coffee makers are a good option. These machines allow you to make a single-serve cup of coffee with little effort. They have a simple interface with an LED indicator that displays how long the coffee will take to brew. A double-wall carafe means that your coffee stays hot longer. It also avoids destroying compounds in your coffee with hot plates.

The temperature of the water you use for brewing can make a big difference in the taste of your drink. The optimal temperature is around 195 degrees Fahrenheit. If your machine is not able to reach that temperature, you can end up with a weak cup of coffee.

Keurig is a household name in the coffee world. While they are simple and convenient, these single-serve coffee machines don't make the best cup of coffee. A Keurig uses pre-ground coffee beans that lose their freshness quickly.

Another type of coffee maker is an automatic coffee machine. It uses a direct water line to brew the coffee and eliminates the need for constantly filling the water reservoir. These machines are great for self-serve at private events or for large crowds. A pourover coffee machine, on the other hand, does not need a direct water line. Pourover machines are portable and don't require any major plumbing procedures or major installation.

CHAPTER 5:
Ways of Making Coffee

There are various ways to make coffee through machines. The most common mechanism is placing coffee in a filter over a pot and either passing water through the filter or dipping the filter in water. There are a lot of advancements in coffee-brewing techniques, and new machines are created all the time.

Turkish Coffee

The instrument used for making it is called "cezve" or "ibrik" and is made of copper or brass. It has a long handle. A brass grinder is used to make a fine powder from coffee beans, which is then used to make coffee. It is served in small cups.

Method of Preparation:

- 50 ml (1.7 ounces) of water per cup of coffee is added to the cezve.
- Then sugar to taste is added and blended by stirring.
- Cezve is then placed on the stove to boil, and a teaspoon of ground coffee is added per cup of coffee.
- Upon boiling, it is immediately removed from the stove and mixed well with help of a spoon to remove the foam.
- Then it is boiled a second time.
- After this, it is kept aside to settle the coffee powder in the base of the cezve and then served in small cups.

French Press

The French press method uses a cylindrical pot with a built-in filter for holding ground coffee. The technique focuses mainly in grinding the coffee because it cannot be too finely ground and pass through the filter or not too coarse and choke the filter.

Method of Preparation:

- First, the pot is held in hand, and plunger is taken out from it.
- Then the coffee powder (7-8 grams) is added per 200ml (6.7 ounces) of water.
- Next, hot water is poured and stirred evenly. The water should not be boiling.
- The plunger is then inserted back into the pot and held just above the water level and is left sitting like this for 3 to 4 minutes.
- Then the plunger is pressed downward with slow and uniform pressure.
- A dry pot is used for making coffee every time.

Geyser Coffee Maker

The Geyser coffee maker is a machine for making coffee also called Moka geyser, Moka Pot, and a caffettiera. It consists of two chambers. The lower cup is filled with water before making coffee, and the upper tank fills itself with coffee while making the drink. There is a filter in the lower tank which is filled with coffee.

Method of Preparation

- First, detach both chambers from each other.

- Fill the lower cup of the Moka pot with boiled water.
- Put coffee in the lower cup filter chamber.
- Reassemble both cups and place it on the heat.
- The coffee will start to trickle into the upper chamber.
- Pour into cups immediately before coffee becomes diluted.

Instant Coffee Production

Instant coffee production starts by roasting coffee beans. Then these roasted beans are finely ground and treated with hot water and high pressure which extracts the water-soluble components from the powdered beans. These water-soluble compounds are refrigerated for cooling and passed through a centrifuge. To increase concentration, it is heated and dried by freezing in order to reduce the moisture to a minimum of 5 percent.

Another method is spray-drying in which high temperature and pressure are used to convert the liquid extract into vapors. Then hot air is passed through the vapors to dehydrate the small drops, which are powdered. This process uses low temperatures for sublimation of frozen liquid extract. This direct conversion of solid to gaseous state produces a higher quality final product in comparison to other methods.

The instant coffee grains are re-wet by using steam, water, or oil and then dried again. This process is known as agglomeration. Robusta coffee beans are generally used in larger percentage for making instant coffee because of the higher number of soluble compounds found in it.

CHAPTER 6:
Tips and Tricks

Tips and Tricks to Make the Perfect Coffee

1. To make your coffee experience more pleasurable, here are some tips to guide you in creating that perfect coffee blend:

2. Always buy fresh roasted and quality coffee beans. Keep them away from bright light and exposure to oxygen.

3. If you want to retain its freshness and aroma, your coffee should be stored in a cool, dark, and actually dry place in an air-tight sealed container. NO to refrigerating or freezing of coffee beans because it can lose its delicate taste and aroma.

4. Store whole coffee beans. Grinding your coffee ahead of time can lose its freshness and flavor.

5. Brew your coffee with a clean paper filter.

6. Use bottled spring water in brewing your coffee. Do not use tap water with chlorine or softened water.

7. When brewing coffee, follow the recommended coffee and water ratio. Water temperature is equally important; it should be 200 F.

8. Reheating, boiling, or using a warmer for a more extended period can lose the pleasant flavor and aroma of your coffee.

9. Keep all your equipment clean; they should be free from oily deposits and mineral build-ups.

10. When making iced coffee beverages, use coffee ice cubes made of brewed coffee instead of plain ice cubes made of water. It will give you better results.

11. When making hot coffee, preheat your cup or mug as it will lengthen the time that your coffee stays warm.

Mistakes to Avoid When Making Coffee

Coffee is a popular beverage, and preparing a cup appears to be a simple operation, but why isn't it the same as going to your favorite coffee shop? There are several reasons for this; errors are frequently made by coffee enthusiasts worldwide, affecting their results.

The art of preparing coffee is less about the fancy devices available and more about your skill. If you avoid the most common errors, you can have a beautiful morning coffee every day.

- **Pouring into a cold cup**

If you pour your coffee into a cold container, the contents will not stay hot for long. Your coffee will stay hot for much longer if you pre-warm it. Pouring some water into your cup before it reaches full boil is an excellent technique to do this. Allow it to sit until the coffee has brewed before emptying it and refilling it with new coffee. This will heat your cup to the ideal temperature, allowing you to enjoy your fresh coffee for a longer period of time.

- **Using old beans**

Use beans that have been roasted within the last three weeks for the finest flavor. Check the roast date, which is usually located on a label or stamped on the package. Stale beans lose their inherent flavor that fresh beans have, resulting in a more blander coffee that looks drab, especially darker roasts. If you don't know the roast date, simply grind a little amount and smell it to determine the status.

- **Using water that isn't fresh**

When making coffee, you should constantly examine the quality of the water you use because it has a significant role. The minerals and contaminants in tap water might make your coffee taste unpleasant. The flavor and aroma of your coffee can be affected by both hard and soft water. Always use pure or filtered water for a pleasant flavor.

- **Clean your coffee making equipment frequently**

Making coffee necessitates the use of several instruments and equipment. It is critical to clean them on a regular basis to guarantee that your coffee remains fresh. This appears to be a simple task, but many people believe it is unnecessary to clean the equipment right before using it again. However, it is critical to clean the equipment as soon as you use it to remove the grease and oils that are present in the coffee, which can leave a bitter taste if not removed.

- **The water to coffee ratio**

The coffee-to-water ratio is critical to grasp in order to make the perfect cup; it also defines your strength. 2 tablespoons of coffee for every 6 ounces of water is the standard 'golden' ratio here. Individual taste preferences can be accommodated. Check the instructions that came with your brewing equipment to see how they measure, and keep in mind that some water can be lost due to evaporation in certain ways.

- **Not using enough coffee**

If you're estimating measurements, you're probably underestimating. Most individuals consume less coffee per cup than is necessary for a variety of reasons, including trying to stretch resources. Being frugal with your resources might result in a bitter and watery cup; if you want a weaker cup, use extra hot water instead of brewing with fewer beans. Everyone has different strength preferences, so experiment with different roasts to discover a flavor that suits you.

- **Masking the bitter taste**

Some individuals prefer to drink their coffee with milk and sugar to eliminate the 'bitter' flavor, which occurs only when the coffee is prepared wrongly! When individuals say the coffee is bitter, they usually indicate that it is excessively strong for them. Try a freshly ground or flawlessly made coffee without any frills (or calories), and you may find that you don't need to add milk or sugar. You'll be surprised to see that the bitter flavor you've been trying to disguise has vanished!

CHAPTER 7:

Coffee Recipes

Ounces	Grams
1/4	7
1/2	15
1	30
2	55
3	85
4	115
5	140
6	170
7	200
8	225
9	255
10	285
11	310
12	340
13	370
14	395
15	425
16	455

1. Almond Espresso Float

Cold espresso coffee rich in almond flavor and ice cream can be the best party drink for a birthday or anniversary celebration. Try this amazing recipe and enjoy.

Serving Size: 1

Preparation Time: 10 minutes

Ingredients:

- ½ tablespoon of water
- 1 teaspoon of Roast Instant Coffee
- ¾ cup of chocolate milk
- Almond extract to taste
- ½ tablespoon of cream soda
- 2 scoops of coffee ice cream
- 2 tablespoons of whipped cream

Directions:

1. Chill a tall glass in the freezer.
2. Mix instant coffee in hot water.
3. Put the prepared coffee mixture, almond extract, and chocolate milk in the glass.
4. Stir all components in the glass to blend thoroughly.
5. Add ice cream.
6. Add cream soda and stir the components.
7. Top with whipped cream.

2. Banana Milk Iced Coffee

People go crazy after bananas or banana milkshakes. So, why not mix it with your coffee? Banana milk iced coffee is a treat to everyone's taste buds. This is a very good combination of tasty fruit and coffee. This iced coffee is very filling, all thanks to the bananas. Regular coffees will not taste as good as this.

Serving Size: 2

Preparation Time: 5 minutes

Ingredients:

- 1 cup of milk
- 1 overripe banana
- 1 tablespoon of sugar or honey
- ice cubes as per requirement
- 1 cup of chilled brew coffee

Directions:

1. Bring out your food blender or mixer. Add the banana and milk in it along with the sugar or honey.
2. Blend till nice and smooth and no banana lumps are left.
3. Bring out your serving glasses and fill them with ice as per your liking. Pour the coffee equally into the glasses.
4. Pour the banana-flavored milk over, give it a good single stir and serve.

3. Bicerin Coffee

Bicerin coffee was first introduced in Italy in 1763 as a celebration drink for victory on French at Saint-Quentin. It provides a joyous feeling and sense of pride.

Serving Size: 2

Preparation Time: 5 minutes

Ingredients:

- 1 cup of whole milk
- 3 ounces of chocolate
- 2 shots of espresso
- 4 tablespoons of whipped cream for topping

Directions:

1. Take a large-sized saucepan.
2. Mix milk and chocolate in it and heat until it boils.
3. Keep mixing while boiling for approximately about 1 minute.
4. Pour this mixture into a transparent glass about 1/3 of the glass.
5. Now pour shots of espresso.
6. Top with whipped cream and enjoy.

4.   Caramel Apple Spice Coffee

This caramel apple spice coffee will tickle your taste buds and you will ask for another cup.

Serving Size: 1

Preparation Time: 10 minutes

Ingredients:

- ½ cup of espresso, cold
- 1 cup of apple juice
- 5 ice cubes
- 3 tablespoons of caramel sauce
- ¼ cup of heavy whipping cream
- 1 tablespoon of powdered sugar
- Pinch of cinnamon
- 1 tablespoon of caramel sauce for serving

Directions:

- Add the cold espresso, apple juice, and caramel sauce to a serving glass filled with ice.
- Mix until combined.
- Whip the whipping cream and powdered sugar with a hand mixer and decorate the glass with the whipped cream.
- Decorate the glass with an additional pinch of ground cinnamon and drizzle of caramel sauce.

5.   Raspberry Iced Coffee

Fruity flavor with coffee is always a good idea. Especially when it comes to raspberries—they pair great with coffee.

Serving Size: 1

Preparation Time: 10 minutes

Ingredients:

- ½ cup of brewed espresso, cold
- 5 ice cubes
- ½ cup of raspberries
- 2 tablespoons of sugar
- 1 teaspoon of vanilla extract

Directions:

1. Add the cold espresso to a serving glass and top it with ice cubes and vanilla.
2. Blitz the raspberries and sugar in a high-speed blender. Strain through a fine-mesh sieve.
3. Pour the raspberry liquid into the glass with the coffee. Serve and enjoy.

6.   Caramel Brulee Latte

This French-inspired coffee is super delicious. It's easy to make at home and super enjoyable with friends and family.

Serving Size: 1

Preparation Time: 10 minutes

Ingredients:

- ½ cup of espresso, cold
- ½ cup of cream
- 5 ice cubes
- 2 tablespoons of caramel sauce
- ¼ cup of heavy whipping cream
- 1 tablespoon of caramel sauce for serving

Directions:

1. Add the cold espresso, cream, ice cubes, and caramel sauce to a blender and blitz until smooth.
2. Transfer to a serving glass.
3. Whip the whipping cream and caramel sauce with a hand mixer and decorate the glass with the whipped cream.
4. Decorate the glass with an additional drizzle of caramel sauce.

7. Caramel Macchiato Frappe

The creamy caramel macchiato frappe recipe is here to your summer delight. It combines coffee, vanilla, and caramel taste.

Serving Size: 1

Preparation Time: 15 minutes

Ingredients:

- 1 teaspoon of Roast Coffee
- 1 tablespoon of water
- 1/3 cup of condensed chocolate milk
- Sugar to taste
- Vanilla extract to taste
- 2 tablespoons of caramel topping
- 6 small ice cubes
- 2 tablespoons of whipped cream

Directions:

1. Mix hot water and coffee.
2. Put all the prepared ingredients except whipped cream in a blender.
3. Blend until mixed.
4. Pour into a prepared glass and top with whipped cream.
5. Add caramel over the topping.
6. Put ice cubes and enjoy!

8.   Chocolate Iced Coffee

This iced coffee is perfect for all the chocolate lovers out there. It is almost impossible to hate this chocolate iced coffee. No matter how foul your mood is, the drink is sure to bring a smile to your face. From children to grumpy grandpas, everyone loved the taste of this coffee. So, go ahead, read through the recipe, follow the instructions and make the wonderful coffee.

Serving Size: 2

Preparation Time: 5 minutes

Ingredients:

- 16 ounces of cold brew coffee
- 2 tablespoons of chocolate syrup
- 1 cup of milk
- 1 cup of ice cubes
- ½ cup of chocolate chips
- whipped cream as a topping

Directions:

1. Make your cold-brewed black coffee according to your preference and taste.
2. Fill the prepared glasses with ice and add the cold coffee over the ice cubes.
3. Pour in the milk equally into two serving glasses and give it a stir.
4. Melt 3/4 cup of the chocolate chips over a saucepan with boiling water. Or microwave the chips till they melt, do not burn the chocolate.
5. Pour the melted chocolate into the glasses equally and give the coffee a few good stirs.
6. Add whipped cream, remaining choco chips. Decorate the cream with chocolate syrup and serve immediately.

9. Cinnamon Dolce Latte

This delicious cinnamon flavored coffee is super easy to make and it's bursting with flavor.

Serving Size: 1

Preparation Time: 10 minutes

Ingredients:

- ¾ cup of boiling water
- 2 teaspoons of instant espresso powder
- ½ cup of milk
- ¼ teaspoon of ground cinnamon
- ¼ teaspoon of nutmeg
- ½ tablespoon powdered sugar
- ¼ cup of heavy whipping cream
- Pinch of cinnamon

Directions:

1. Add the prepared boiling water and espresso powder to a serving glass.
2. Mix and stir in the milk, ground cinnamon, and nutmeg.
3. Whip the whipping cream and powdered sugar and top the glass with whipped cream.
4. Decorate with a pinch of cinnamon.

10. Coconut Oil Coffee

Are you in need of a coffee recipe that is unique and tasty? This Coconut Oil coffee is for you. Try this refreshing ice coffee recipe and you will enjoy every sip.

Serving Size: 2

Preparation Time: 5 minutes

Ingredients:

- 1 ½ cups of brewed coffee
- ¼ teaspoon of ground cinnamon
- 3 teaspoons of coconut oil
- 4 ounces of coconut milk, unsweetened
- 1 tablespoon of whipping cream

For seasoning:

- ¼ teaspoon of cayenne pepper

Directions:

1. Pour coffee in a blender, add coconut oil and then blend for 1 minute or more until frothy.
2. Add remaining ingredients except for cream and pulse for 20 seconds until blended.
3. Divide coffee between two mugs, top each mug with a tbsp of whipping cream and then serve.

11. Espresso Martini

Aside from coffee, do you also love martini? If your answer is yes, then you will simply love this espresso martini.

Serving Size: 1

Preparation Time: 5 minutes

Ingredients:

- A handful of ice cubes
- ¼ teaspoon of white sugar
- 1 cup of espresso, brewed, dark roast
- 3 tablespoons of vodka, preferred
- 3 tablespoons of Kahlua (coffee liquor)

Directions:

1. Using a drip coffeemaker with a filter, brew espresso beans.
2. Meanwhile using a cocktail shaker, fill it up with ice cubes.
3. Pour the brewed espresso, vodka, sugar, and Kahlua then shake together until it becomes foamy.
4. Strain contents to a martini glass and serve immediately.

12. Gingerbread Latte

This ground ginger coffee will tickle your taste buds and you will ask for another cup.

Serving Size: 1

Preparation Time: 10 minutes

Ingredients:

- ½ cup of espresso, cold
- 1 cup of milk
- 5 ice cubes
- 2 tablespoons of simple syrup
- ½ teaspoon of ground cinnamon
- ½ teaspoon of ground ginger
- ¼ teaspoon of ground nutmeg
- ¼ cup of heavy whipping cream
- Pinch of ground ginger

Directions:

1. Add the cold espresso, cream, ice cubes, simple syrup, cinnamon, ginger, and nutmeg to a blender and blitz until smooth. Transfer to a serving glass.
2. Whip the prepared whipping cream with a hand mixer or wire whisk and decorate the glass with the whipped cream.
3. Decorate the glass with an additional pinch of ground ginger.

13. Honey and Molasses Coffee

This recipe blends golden honey, pure molasses and spices with coffee. It creates a comforting warm beverage especially suited for cold days.

Serving Size: 4

Preparation Time: 25 minutes

Ingredients:

- 1/2 cup of coffee, ground
- 1 & 1/2 cups of water, cold
- 1 & 1/3 cups of milk, 2%
- 2 tablespoons of honey, pure
- 2 tablespoons of molasses, organic
- 4 teaspoons of sugar, granulated
- 1/4 teaspoon of ginger, ground
- 1/4 teaspoon of cinnamon, ground
- 1/8 teaspoon of nutmeg, ground
- 1/8 teaspoon of cloves, ground
- Optional, for topping: whipped cream, sweetened

Directions:

- Place the coffee in drip coffee maker filter. Add the water. Brew using directions of manufacturer.
- In small-sized pan, combine milk, molasses, honey, spices & sugar. Stir while cooking on med. heat till it steams. Remove from heat. Transfer to food processor. Process till foamy, approximately about 15 seconds.
- Divide into 4 mugs and add coffee. Use whipped cream to top, if you like. Serve.

14. Horchata Latte

Horchata latte is a unique coffee recipe that takes a long time to make but the wait is working the taste. It contains a mesmerizing flavor of rice and cinnamon.

Serving Size: 3

Preparation Time: 10 minutes

Ingredients:

- 1 cup of brewed Folgers Gourmet Natural Caramel
- 1 cup of white rice
- 2 cups of water
- 1 cup of almond milk
- 1 ½ teaspoons of cinnamon powder
- 2 tablespoons of honey
- 4 ice cubes

Directions:

- Blend water, almond milk, rice and cinnamon in a blender. Do not blend too much.
- Pour the prepared mixture into a large-sized bowl and add 1 cup of brewed coffee. Leave it for approximately about 3 hours at room temperature.
- In a large-sized pan, simmer honey at low heat until its color become light amber.
- Now, remove from heat and cool at room temperature.
- Pour honey mixture and coffee-rice mixture again in a blender and blend until mixed.
- Strain the mixture through a mesh sieve.
- Put ice cubes and enjoy.

15. Hot Butter Coffee

Your spirits will be warmed up indeed because of the richness of this coffee.

Serving Size: 20

Preparation Time: 15 minutes

Ingredients:

- 1/2 teaspoon of ground cinnamon
- 1/4 teaspoon of ground allspice
- 1 cup of packed brown sugar
- 1/4 cup of softened butter
- 1/4 teaspoon of ground nutmeg
- 1 teaspoon of vanilla extract
- 1/8 teaspoon of ground cloves

For serving:

- 1 cup of hot French or other dark roast brewed coffee
- Cinnamon sticks, whipped cream (optional)

Directions:

1. Mix all the prepared ingredients in a small bowl until blended. Transfer in an airtight container and store it in the fridge for approximately about up to 2 weeks.
2. To prepare the drink, put a tbsp of the spice mixture in a mug. Add hot coffee. Serve with the optional ingredients if you want.

16. Iced Coconut Caramel Coffee

Coconut milk is very smooth and tasty to have. It is naturally sweet that is neither subtle nor overpowering. Just the right amount of natural saccharin. And it goes very well with coffee as well. And caramel, without a doubt, just adds more flavor to this coffee. It is a very good iced coffee with unique combinations. Follow and read through the recipe along with its instructions to make the perfect drink.

Serving Size: 2

Preparation Time: 5 minutes

Ingredients:

- 12 ounces of chilled brewed coffee
- 2 ounces of coconut milk
- 2 tablespoons of caramel syrup
- Whipped cream to garnish
- Ice cubes as per requirements

Directions:

1. Bring out two serving glasses and add a tablespoon of caramel syrup into each glass.
2. Fill each glass with ice to the level of your liking. Now divide the chilled coffee equally between the two glasses.
3. Pour in a tablespoon of coconut milk into each of the glasses. Stir all of the ingredients well together.
4. Whip some cream above the coffee drinks and serve chilled. For extra decorative visuals, dust some coffee powder over the whipped cream.

17. Iced Mint Coffee

If you want a cool and mint flavor yet a strong drink, then this iced mint coffee is for you. Try this refreshing ice coffee recipe and enjoy your mornings.

Serving Size: 2

Preparation Time: 10 minutes

Ingredients:

- ¼ cup of Folgers Mint Flavored Ground Coffee
- 2 cups of chilled water
- ½ tablespoon of mint jelly
- 1 tablespoon of brown sugar
- 6 fresh mint leaves
- 6 ice cubes
- 1 cup of whipped cream

Directions:

1. Brew 1 cup of coffee from 1 ½ cups of chilled water.
2. Pour coffee into a jar along with mint jelly and mix until the jelly is melted down.
3. Now put a half cup of water in the jar and mix again.
4. Take a bowl and mix brown sugar and whipped cream.
5. Pour coffee mixture into glasses and pour sugar cream mixture on top.
6. Add ice cubes and place mint leaves on top.

18. Indian Cappuccino

Indian cappuccino is another version of legendary cappuccino coffee with some added spices to enhance its feel and taste. Try this rich taste cappuccino.

Serving Size: 2

Preparation Time: 10 minutes

Ingredients:

- 1 tablespoon of instant coffee
- 1 ½ cup of condensed milk
- ¼ cinnamon
- ¼ ground nutmeg
- ½ cup of water

Directions:

- Put instant coffee, cinnamon and ground nutmeg in a cup.
- Add 1 tablespoon water and stir well until instant coffee turns into a thick paste.
- Divide equally the paste into two cups.
- Now pour milk and half cup water in a pan on heat.
- Fill the two cups with this hot milk.
- Stir well to mix the coffee-and-spicy paste and milk.
- Sprinkle coffee powder on top and enjoy.

19. Minty Mojito Iced Coffee

Minty Mojito Iced Coffee definitely deserves more attention. Although we do understand that mint and coffee might be weird to some, regardless, it is a combination worth giving a try. The cool minty flavor is worth giving a shot. Bring out all the ingredients and make some simple iced coffee for you and your loved ones at home.

Serving Size: 1

Preparation Time: 10 minutes

Ingredients:

- 1 cup of strong brewed coffee
- 12 large mint leaves (extra to garnish, optional)
- 1 tablespoon of sugar or honey
- 1 cup of ice cubes
- splash of cream that you prefer

Directions:

1. Brew and make the coffee in the method you prefer.
2. Bring out a cocktail shaker, and add the fresh mint leaves to it. Muddle the leaves till it releases its juices.
3. Fill the shaker with ice and add coffee into the shaker.
4. Cover the shaker with its lid and shake well for a few seconds until the whole drink is chilled.
5. Strain the minty coffee and keep it aside. Bring out your serving glass.
6. Add the cream and pour in the minty coffee over it. Stir and mix well.
7. Now, add the sugar or honey and give it a few more good stirs. Garnish with the extra mint leaves and serve immediately.

20. Mocha Frappuccino

Decadent, delicious, and super easy to make. Let your next morning coffee be different and much tastier.

Serving Size: 1

Preparation Time: 10 minutes

Ingredients:

- ¾ cup of strongly brewed espresso, cold
- ½ cup of whole milk
- 3 tablespoons of chocolate sauce
- 5 ice cubes
- ¼ cup of heavy whipping cream
- 1 teaspoon of powdered sugar

Directions:

1. Add the prepared whipping cream and powdered sugar to a bowl and whip them with a hand mixer until stiff peaks form.
2. Combine the espresso, milk, and chocolate sauce in a big glass.
3. Add the ice cubes and mix thoroughly.
4. Decorate the top of the glass with the whipped cream.
5. Drizzle some extra fudge on top.

21. Nutmeg Holiday Coffee

This Nutmeg Holiday Coffee combines all the memorable flavors of the holiday and the distinct morning coffee taste.

Serving Size: 2

Preparation Time: 7 minutes

Ingredients:

- 2 tablespoons of instant coffee
- 2 cups of water
- ½ of a cinnamon stick
- 1 tablespoon of sugar, adjust to desired sweetness
- ¼ teaspoon of nutmeg
- 1 clove
- 1 teaspoon of orange zest

Directions:

1. Add all your ingredients over medium heat in a saucepan, then allow to simmer for about 2 minutes. Stir continuously.
2. Turn heat off and steep for 4 minutes. Strain before serving.

22. Peppermint Patty Coffee

Peppermint patty coffee is a very delicious coffee with a mint flavor, which gives a soothing effect while taking sips. This recipe provides the perfect combination of coffee and mint.

Serving Size: 1

Preparation Time: 10 minutes

Ingredients:

- 8 ounces of strong brewed coffee
- 2 tablespoons of cocoa powder
- 2 ounces of heavy milk
- ½ teaspoon of peppermint extract
- Sugar to taste

Directions:

- Put the dry ingredients in a regular cup.
- Pour hot coffee from above.
- Add peppermint extract.
- Stir to dissolve all ingredients.
- Serve and enjoy.

23. Pour-Over Classic Coffee

Making coffee with the pour-over method is a quaint and nostalgic way to brew coffee. It creates a flavorful and rich coffee. You need to precisely measure and watch your exact brewing times, but no unusual equipment is needed to make this wonderful drink.

Serving Size: 1

Preparation Time: 20 minutes

Ingredients:

- 2/3 ounces of coffee, med-fine grind
- 10 ounces of water, filtered or distilled

Directions:

- Pour heated water in cup you'll be using to serve, so it warms up.
- Add water to kettle. Heat on stove till temperature is between 195F & 205F.
- Grind the coffee beans into med. or fine ground.
- Measure ground coffee in pour over brewer.
- When all water has heated, dump water from cup filled above. Set drip cone on rim of cup.
- Zero out scale. Start your timer. Start in middle of coffee grounds & work around, pouring just the right amount of water to wet all coffee, about 1 & 3/4 fluid ounces. Allow it to bloom, saturating coffee for approximately about 30 to 45 seconds.
- Continue slowly pouring water over coffee ground bed. Working in even circles, start in center and move outwards. Pour water into coffee grounds only, not into filter or cone. Pause if you need to, till all 10 oz. of water have been used.
- Your goal is a total time brewing of approximately about 3-4 minutes if you like your coffee medium roast, or 2 & 1/2 – 3 minutes if you prefer dark roast. Expect it to continue dripping for approximately about 1/2 minute after all water has been added.
- Tap cone, releasing all coffee bits. Set on saucer so it can catch additional drips, if any. Serve.

24. Pumpkin and Spice Latte

This is America's favorite autumn coffee, made more popular by a famous coffee chain. It's just as tasty and less expensive to make it at home.

Serving Size: 1

Preparation Time: 15 minutes

Ingredients:

- 1 cup of milk, 2%
- 2 tablespoons of pumpkin puree, unsweetened
- 1 tablespoon of sugar, granulated, +/- as desired
- 1 teaspoon of cinnamon, ground
- 1/2 teaspoon of ginger, ground
- 1/4 teaspoon of nutmeg, ground
- 1/8 teaspoon of cloves, ground
- 1/2 teaspoon of vanilla, pure
- 1/2 cup of espresso, brewed

For Toppings:

- whipped cream, sweetened, as desired

Directions:

1. Add pumpkin puree, cinnamon, sugar, nutmeg, ginger, vanilla, cloves & espresso to small-sized pot.
2. Bring to simmer over med-low heat. Occasionally whisk till puree is incorporated well and spices and sugar have dissolved.
3. Add milk to separate pot. Heat till warmed through.
4. Vigorously whisk milk till it starts frothing or foaming.
5. Pour heated coffee mixture into mug. Add frothy milk. Top as desired. Serve.

25. Vanilla Iced Coffee

Vanilla iced coffee is one of the simplest iced coffee to exist. The subtle taste of vanilla and its aroma are always soothing. It is a simple beverage loved by most, and it easily refreshes you up. It doesn't even take time to make. Vanilla iced coffee works for the type of people who do not like overpowering flavors. Follow the recipe carefully and enjoy a tasty cup of iced vanilla coffee.

Serving Size: 1

Preparation Time: 10 minutes

Ingredients:

- 1/2 cup of any milk
- 1/2 cup of strong brewed coffee
- 1/4 teaspoon of vanilla extract or more
- sweetener of your choice, optional
- Ice as per requirement

Directions:

1. Pour the milk, sweetener, and vanilla extract into a shaker or a jar with a lid. Shake for 3 minutes till it is foamy.
2. Place the milk in the microwave for half a minute. Meanwhile, Make your cold-brewed coffee as per your liking.
3. Allow the coffee to cool to some temperate. Fill your serving cup with ice to the level you prefer.
4. Transfer the coffee into your serving cup. Using a spoon, pour the milk slowly into the cup. Restrict the froth from entering the cup.
5. Scoop out the froth and place it over the iced coffee and serve.

26. Vienna Coffee

The traditional Vienna coffee is prepared from brewed coffee and whipped cream instead of milk and sugar. The sip of coffee comes through the cream and gives a delightful taste.

Serving Size: 2

Preparation Time: 7 minutes

Ingredients:

- 2 cups of brewed coffee
- ½ cup of whipped cream
- 1 tablespoon of chocolate syru
- 2 tablespoons of Irish cream liqueur
- Sugar as per taste

Directions:

1. Take a slow cooker.
2. Add coffee, sugar and chocolate syrup.
3. Cover the cooker and leave on low heat for 2.5 hours.
4. After this mix heavy cream and Irish cream liqueur.
5. Close lid and cook again for half an hour.
6. Now, serve in cups.
7. Garnish with whipped cream.

27. Viennese Mexican Coffee

If you enjoy adding spices and herbs to your meal, this coffee recipe is something you should not miss. It is perfect if you crave something different for your coffee. The combination of fruit and chocolate flavors of South American drinks and the spiciness of Viennese coffee will give your taste buds a different experience.

Serving Size: 4

Preparation Time: 10 minutes

Ingredients:

- 4 cups of hot brewed coffee
- ¼ cup of heavy whipping cream
- ¾ cup of whole milk
- 2 tablespoons of brown sugar
- 4 teaspoons of cocoa powder
- 2 teaspoons of orange extract
- 2 teaspoons of vanilla extract
- 2 teaspoons of ground cinnamon
- ½ teaspoon of ground nutmeg
- ½ teaspoon of ground cloves

Directions:

- Combine the coffee, cream, milk, vanilla extract, brown sugar, orange extract, cocoa powder, nutmeg, cinnamon, and cloves in a large cup until it actually becomes smooth.

28. White Chocolate Mocha

If you are actually a white chocolate lover, then this smooth and nice chilled coffee is everything you need to keep you on your feet for the day.

Serving Size: 1

Preparation Time: 10 minutes

Ingredients:

- ½ cup of brewed strong espresso, hot
- 2 ounces of white chocolate, chopped
- ½ cup of milk
- 5 ice cubes
- ¼ cup of heavy whipping cream
- 1 teaspoon of sugar
- Pinch of nutmeg

Directions:

1. Add the white chocolate to the hot espresso and let it melt.
2. Stir in the cold milk and pour the mixture into a serving glass filled with ice cubes.
3. Use a hand mixer to whip the whipping cream and sugar.
4. Decorate the serving glass with whipped cream and sprinkle with nutmeg.

29. Creamed Belgian Coffee

Serving Size: 1

Preparation Time: 5 minutes

Ingredients:

- 2 shots of espresso
- 1 fluid ounces of Belgian cookie syrup
- 2 ounces of whipped cream
- Dark chocolate, grated

Directions:

- In a serving cup, stir together the espresso and Belgian cookie syrup.
- Serve with whipped cream and dark chocolate on top.

30. White Russian Coffee

The base for this coffee is leftover coffee grounds, and they create a new twist on a classic cocktail with coffee. I used a bit of vodka that is blended with rum, cream and vanilla.

Serving Size: 4

Preparation Time: 25 minutes

Ingredients:

- 3 tablespoons of coffee grounds, used
- 1 cup of rum, dark
- 2 tablespoons of syrup, maple
- Ice, for mixing
- 1 pod of vanilla
- 5 ounces of cream, double
- 5 ounces of vodka, milk

Directions:

- Add coffee grounds to bowl or jar. Pour rum over the top. Cover. Allow 24 hours of steeping time.
- Next day, strain rum into jug through a fine sieve. Stir in maple syrup.
- Pour coffee rum evenly into four glasses. Top with cubed ice. In jug, mix seeds from pod of vanilla together with vodka and double cream.
- Place spoon atop ice in glass. Pour 1/4 of boozy cream slowly onto spoon. Allow cream to overflow into glass. This helps the layer of cream to float atop coffee liqueur.
- Repeat with last three glasses. Serve with stirrers.

31. Iced Ube Milky Coffee

Serving Size: 6

Preparation Time: 10 minutes

Ingredients:

- 16 ounces of almond milk
- 16 ounces of rice milk
- ¼ cup of granulated sugar
- 16 ounces of coconut milk
- 2 teaspoons of ground cinnamon
- 3 teaspoons of ube (yam) extract
- 1 shot Espresso
- Ice, crushed, for mixing and serving

Directions:

- In a large pitcher, pour milk, then gradually add sugar and cinnamon, keep mixing quickly to avoid forming.
- Once everything is mixed through, add ube extract, and mix until blended completely.
- Pour some ice in the serving glass, add ube mixture until nearly full, and serve with 1 shot of espresso on top.

32. Coffee Vanilla Milkshake

Serving Size: 1

Preparation Time: 5 minutes

Ingredients:

- 2 scoops of vanilla ice cream, divided
- 2/3 cup of skim milk
- 2 shots of espresso, cooled
- 5-6 cubes of ice

Directions:

- In a high-speed blender, add 1 scoop of ice cream, espresso, skim milk, and ice. Blend until mixture becomes consistent and smooth.
- Once done, pour the blended coffee mixture into a chilled serving glass. Serve with the reserved scoop of ice cream on top.

33. Irish Coffee Milkshake

Serving Size: 1

Preparation Time: 5 minutes

Ingredients:

- 2 teaspoons of sugar
- ½ cup of milk
- ½ cup of low fat yogurt
- 1 teaspoon of coffee granules
- 1 teaspoon of Irish whiskey
- Ice cubes, as needed

Directions:

- In a blender, add sugar, milk, yogurt, coffee granules, whiskey and ice.
- Blend all the ingredients on low speed for 60 seconds.
- Once desired smoothness is achieved, transfer to the serving glass with extra ice cubes and serve!

34. Cinnamon and Honey Latte

Serving Size: 1

Preparation Time: 5 minutes

Ingredients:

- 2 ounces of espresso
- 2 teaspoons of honey, + more for garnish
- ½ teaspoon of vanilla extract
- ¼ teaspoon of ground cinnamon, + more for garnish
- 10 ounces of milk

Directions:

- Transfer the espresso into a mug, add vanilla, honey and ground cinnamon, mix well.
- Pour milk in your saucepan over moderate heat. Remove just before milk starts to boil.
- Make froth using a frother for around 20 to 30 seconds.
- Twist your glass and gently tap on the counter until large bubbles start to appear.
- Hold back foam using the back of a spoon, and add milk into your espresso. Top the coffee with remaining foam, cinnamon and honey, serve immediately.

35. Butterscotch Latte

Serving Size: 1

Preparation Time: 5 minutes

Ingredients:

- 2 tablespoons of butterscotch sauce
- ¼ cup of cream
- ½ cup of espresso
- 1 tablespoon of molasses
- 1 tablespoon of brown sugar
- ¼ cup of heavy whipping cream
- Pinch of cinnamon

Directions:

- Brew the espresso with your coffee machine.
- Take a serving glass and add the espresso, butterscotch, molasses and whipping cream and mix.
- With a hand mixer mix the whipping cream and the brown sugar and place on top of the serving glass. Top it with cinnamon and serve.

36. Vanilla Milk Espresso Frappe

Serving Size: 1

Preparation Time: 5 minutes

Ingredients:

- 2 ounces of chilled espresso
- 1 cup of vanilla ice cream
- 1 cup of ice
- 4 ounces of milk
- ¼ teaspoon of vanilla extract
- Whipped cream, for garnish

Directions:

- Combine the espresso, ice cream, ice, milk, plus vanilla in your blender, and blend until smooth.
- Serve topped with whipped cream, as desired.

37. Vietnamese Milk Coffee

Serving Size: 1

Preparation Time: 5 minutes

Ingredients:

- 2 tablespoons of sweetened condensed milk
- 3 1/2 teaspoons of ground coffee with chicory
- boiling water, as needed

Directions:

- Pour the condensed milk in your glass, and set aside for a while.
- Steep the coffee grounds in your heatproof container with boiling water within 4 minutes.
- Pour through your coffee filter into your prepared condensed milk glass, and stir well until blended. Serve and enjoy!

38. Paprika Infused Coffee

Serving Size: 1

Preparation Time: 10 minutes

Ingredients:

- ½ teaspoon of paprika powder
- ¾ cup of hot brewed coffee
- 1 tablespoon of heavy cream

Directions:

- Add the brewed coffee to a serving glass and stir in the paprika powder, mix well.
- Then add heavy cream and mix thoroughly. Serve immediately.

39. Peanut Butter Jelly Coffee Smoothie

Serving Size: 2

Preparation Time: 5 minutes

Ingredients:

- 1 cup of cold, strong coffee
- 1 cup of milk, 2% milkfat
- 1 tablespoon of peanut butter
- 4 tablespoons of strawberry jelly

Directions:

- Place coffee, milk, peanut butter and strawberry jelly in a blender, and blend at high speed until foamy.
- Once ready, pour into your glasses and serve.

40. Hot Coffee Masala

Serving Size: 2

Preparation Time: 5 minutes

Ingredients:

- 2 cups of water
- 2 cumin seeds, or to taste
- 1 whole star anise pod
- 1/2 cinnamon stick
- 1 1/2 teaspoon of coffee granules
- 2 teaspoons of nonfat dry milk powder
- 2 teaspoons of white sugar

Directions:

- Boil water in a saucepan; star anise pod, add cinnamon stick, and cumin seeds, then stir. Decrease heat to a simmer; cook while occasionally stirring for 2 to 3 minutes.
- Mix in instant coffee; let the drink simmer gently for another 2 minutes. Transfer the drink to mugs.
- Strain out the spices, add in 1 tsp. of white sugar plus 1 tsp of nonfat dry milk powder in each mug, and stir it well. Serve and enjoy!

41. Hot Buttered Coffee

Serving Size: 20

Preparation Time: 15 minutes

Ingredients:

- 1/8 teaspoon of cloves, ground
- ½ teaspoon of ground cinnamon
- 1 teaspoon of vanilla extract
- ¼ cup of butter, softened
- ¼ teaspoon of allspice, ground
- 1 cup of brown sugar
- ¼ teaspoon of nutmeg, ground

For serving:
- 1 cup of hot brewed coffee (French or another dark roast)
- whipped cream & Cinnamon sticks

Directions:

- In a small bowl, add sugar, butter, cinnamon, vanilla, allspice, nutmeg and cloves, mix thoroughly to prepare spice. You can transfer the spice to an airtight container and reserve in the fridge for 2 weeks.

For hot buttered coffee:
- Add 1 tablespoon of your spice mixture to a mug, then mix in the coffee. Serve with cinnamon stick and whipped cream on top.

42. Orange Mint Coffee

Serving Size: 2

Preparation Time: 5 minutes

Ingredients:

- 2 fresh mint sprigs
- 2 unpeeled fresh orange slices
- 2 cups of hot strong brewed coffee
- 1/3 cup of heavy whipping cream
- 2 teaspoons of sugar

Directions:

- Place a mint sprig and an orange slice in 2 coffee cups. Add hot coffee into cups.
- Beat cream in a small bowl till it forms soft peaks. Add sugar gradually; beat till it forms stiff peaks. Serve with the coffee.

43. Date and Banana Coffee Smoothie

Serving Size: 1

Preparation Time: 5 minutes

Ingredients:

- 4 pitted dates
- 1 frozen banana, peeled, chopped & freeze overnight
- ½ cup of fresh coffee
- ½ cup of soya milk
- ¼ teaspoon of vanilla extract

Directions:

- In a blender, add dates, frozen banana, soya milk, coffee, and vanilla extract.
- Blend until smooth, transfer to your glass and serve.

44. Espresso Macchiato

Serving Size: 1

Preparation Time: 5 minutes

Ingredients:

- 1 cup of hot water
- 1 teaspoon of ground espresso coffee
- 2 tablespoons of milk
- 2–3 tablespoons of hot milk

Directions:

- Brew the espresso in your coffee machine. Add freshly brewed coffee to a glass and add hot milk. Stir.
- Use a milk frother to whip up some milk and use the foam to decorate the glass.

45. Macadamia Mocha Espresso

Serving Size: 1

Preparation Time: 5 minutes

Ingredients:

- 2 shots of espresso
- 1-ounce of macadamia nut syrup
- 1-ounce of chocolate fudge syrup
- ½ cup of steamed milk

Directions:

- Take two shots of coffee in a glass. Add macadamia nut and chocolate fudge syrup.
- Fill the glass with steamed milk, and top with cream or chocolate if desired.

46. Cocoa Powder Espresso

Serving Size: 1

Preparation Time: 5 minutes

Ingredients:

- 1 tablespoon of cocoa powder
- 1 teaspoon of powdered sugar
- ½ cup of brewed coffee, hot
- ¼ cup of whipped cream

Directions:

- Take a serving glass and add the brewed coffee and cocoa powder and stir.
- Use a mixer to whip the whipped cream and powdered sugar. Spoon the mixture over the coffee and serve.

47. Mediterranan Coffee

Serving Size: 8

Preparation Time: 10 minutes

Ingredients:

- 8 cups of strongly brewed coffee
- 1/3 cup of white sugar
- 4 cinnamon sticks
- ¼ cup of chocolate syrup
- ½ teaspoon of aniseed, tied in a cheesecloth
- 1 ½ teaspoon of cloves, whole
- lemon & orange twists for garnishing
- ½ cup of whipped cream for garnishing

Directions:

- In a saucepan over medium-high heat, add sugar, cinnamon sticks, freshly brewed strong coffee, chocolate syrup, aniseed and whole cloves.
- Bring the mixture to boil, then reduce heat and allow to simmer.
- Once ready, strain and pour into mugs, and serve with whipped cream and lemon and orange twists on top.

48. Scandinavian Egg Coffee

Serving Size: 8

Preparation Time: 10 minutes

Ingredients:

- 4-1/2 quarts of water
- 1-1/2 cups of regular grind, Scandinavian or Danish blend coffee
- 1 egg white
- ½ cup of cold water

Directions:

- In a large saucepan, pour 4 ½ quarts of water and bring to boil. In a separate bowl, mix egg white and coffee, reserve egg shell. Add egg shell and coffee-egg mixture into water and bring to boil again.
- Once the mixture start to boil, take off from heat and let it steep for 1 to 2 minutes. To settle the ground, gradually add cold water. Once ready, transfer to the mugs and serve immediately.

49. Black Forest Coffee

Serving Size: 1

Preparation Time: 5 minutes

Ingredients:

- 1 tablespoon of Maraschino cherry juice
- 2 tablespoons of chocolate syrup
- 6 ounces of freshly brewed hot coffee
- Maraschino cherries, as needed
- Whipped cream, as needed
- Shaved chocolate chips as needed

Directions:

- Combine the coffee, chocolate syrup, and cherry juice in your coffee mug, and stir it well.
- Garnish the coffee with whipped cream, then top it with some chocolate shavings plus the Maraschino cherry. Serve and enjoy!

50. Coffee Vanilla Milkshake

Serving Size: 1

Preparation Time: 5 minutes

Ingredients:

- 2 scoops of vanilla ice cream, divided
- 2/3 cup of skim milk
- 2 shots of espresso, cooled
- 5-6 cubes of ice

Directions:

- In a high-speed blender, add 1 scoop of ice cream, espresso, skim milk, and ice. Blend until mixture becomes consistent and smooth.
- Once done, pour the blended coffee mixture into a chilled serving glass. Serve with the reserved scoop of ice cream on top.

51. Cloud Caramello Macchiato

Serving Size: 1

Preparation Time: 5 minutes

Ingredients:

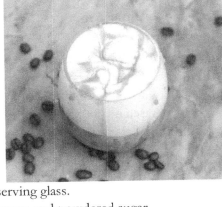

- 1 teaspoon of caramel sauce
- 1 teaspoon of ground espresso coffee
- 1 teaspoon of milk powder
- ½ teaspoon of powdered sugar
- ¼ cup of heavy whipping cream
- ¼ cup of milk

Directions:

- Brew the espresso with your coffee machine and pour it in a serving glass.
- Take a bowl and pour in the milk, powdered milk, whipping cream and powdered sugar.
- Mix the mixture with a hand mixer until you see "peaks" forming.
- Add the mixture on top of the espresso and top everything with the caramel sauce.

52. Birthday Frappuccino

Serving Size: 1

Preparation Time: 5 minutes

Ingredients:

- 2 tablespoons of hazelnut syrup
- vanilla ice cream
- ½ cup of milk
- ½ cup of espresso
- 1 teaspoon of vanilla extract
- 1 tablespoon of sprinkles
- 6 cups of ice cubes

Directions:

- Brew the espresso with your coffee machine.
- Mix the cold espresso, ice cubes, milk, vanilla extract and hazelnut syrup in a blender.
- Place the mixture in a serving glass and top with the vanilla ice cream.
- Add some sprinkles and serve.

53. Avocado Espresso

Serving Size: 1

Preparation Time: 5 minutes

Ingredients:

- ¼ cup of espresso cooled
- ½ avocado
- 2 tablespoons of condensed milk, sweetened
- 1 cup of milk

Directions:

- In a high-speed blender, add milk, condensed milk, espresso and avocado.
- Blend until all the ingredients are mixed through and mixture becomes consistent.
- Once ready, transfer to the serving glass. Drizzle of chocolate syrup on top and serve.

54. Hazelnut Espresso

Serving Size: 1

Preparation Time: 5 minutes

Ingredients:

- 1 tablespoon of grated chocolate
- 1 tablespoon of hazelnut syrup
- 1 teaspoon of ground espresso coffee
- ½ cup of water
- ¼ cup of milk

Directions:

- Pour the brew espresso and milk into a serving glass and stir.
- Now add the hazelnut syrup and stir.
- Top with the grated chocolate and serve.

55. Europe Coffee

Serving Size: 2

Preparation Time: 5 minutes

Ingredients:

- 2 tablespoons of half and half
- ¼ teaspoon of vanilla extract
- 1 egg white
- 1 cup of strong hot coffee (preferably dark roast)

Directions:

- In a bowl, add vanilla and egg white, beat until stiff, then transfer equal portions to two mugs.
- Pour coffee and a half and half on top. Serve immediately.

56. Mint Vanilla Coffee

Serving Size: 4

Preparation Time: 5 minutes

Ingredients:

- 1 cup of cold, strong coffee
- 1 cup of vanilla ice cream
- 1 cup of mint ice cream
- 1 teaspoon of mint extract
- mint leaves for garnish

Directions:

- Place the ice creams, coffee, plus mint extract into your blender, and blend until consistent and smooth.
- Once ready, divide and transfer to the 4 wine glasses and serve with mint leaves on top.

57. Pecan-Maple Latte

Serving Size: 1

Preparation Time: 10 minutes

Ingredients:

For the Syrup:

- 1/3 cup of heavy cream
- 1/2 tablespoon of unsalted butter
- 1/4 cup of maple syrup
- 2 tablespoons of brown sugar
- 1/4 cup of natural peanut butter
- 1 teaspoon of pure vanilla extract,

For the Latte:

- 1 shot of espresso
- 2 tablespoons of pecan-maple syrup
- 1/2 cup of steamed milk,

For the Garnishing:

- Whipped cream, as you like
- chopped pecans, toasted, as you like

Directions:

- In a small pot over medium-high heat, add maple syrup, peanut butter, brown sugar and butter. Stir while cooking for 2 to3 minutes until sugar disappears and dissolves completely.
- Remove the syrup from the heat, add vanilla extract and cream, set aside until completely cooled. This syrup is enough for eight lattes.
- In a mug, add espresso and 2 tbsp. of pecan-maple syrup, mix until blended thoroughly.
- Then add steamed milk, top with the whipped cream and pecans, and serve.

58. Toffee Coffee

The soothing chocolate toffee from this drink can make mornings more pleasant. You can also have it as a treat in the afternoon if you are feeling down.

Serving Size: 5

Preparation Time: 15 minutes

Ingredients:

- 5 cups of hot brewed coffee
- ½ cup of whipping cream
- 1 tablespoon of confectioner's sugar
- ½ cup of milk chocolate toffee bits
- 2 tablespoons of butterscotch ice cream topping

Directions:

- Beat the prepared cream in a small bowl until it starts to become thick.
- Add the confectioner's sugar and beat until stiff peaks are formed.
- Add toffee bits in the coffee and let them sit for approximately about 30 seconds.
- Strain and throw the toffee bits that didn't dissolve.
- Pour the coffee into mugs, put whipped cream on top, and drizzle with the butterscotch topping.

59. Vegan Iced Coffee

We support all healthy lifestyles, including veganism. Those who think vegans are missing out on food and drinks are clearly mistaken. The biggest battle some vegans face is substituting dairy products in their everyday meals and drinks. Thankfully, plant-based milk comes to their rescue. It tastes the same as normal milk, if not better. Follow the recipe given below to make the drink.

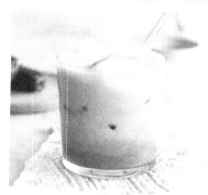

Serving Size: 1

Preparation Time: 5 minutes

Ingredients:

- 2 teaspoons of Instant Espresso Powder
- 1 cup of Hot Water
- 3 tablespoons of Vegan Condensed Milk
- Ice as per requirement
- 1 teaspoon of sugar or agave

Directions:

1. Pour the water into your mixing mug. Add the espresso powder into the mug.
2. Mix the coffee with the hot water by stirring it continuously. Now pour in the vegan condensed milk.
3. Make sure to stir well to combine the ingredients properly together.
4. Add ice all according to your preference. Pour the coffee all over the frozen cubes.
5. Add the sweetener of your choice and stir the coffee a few more times till it dissolves well. Serve the chilled drink immediately.

60. Caramel Affogato

Serving Size: 1

Preparation Time: 5 minutes

Ingredients:

- ¼ cup of warm milk
- 2 scoops of caramel ice cream
- 2 teaspoons of finely ground espresso

Directions:

- Make espresso coffee with your coffee machine and pour it into a container with the caramel ice cream.
- Stir the coffee and ice cream until the latter has melted.
- Add the mixture to a small cup with the hot milk, stir and serve.

61. Tembleque Latte

Serving Size: 1

Preparation Time: 5 minutes

Ingredients:

- 1 shot of brewed espresso
- 1 (1.5 fluid oz.) jigger coconut-flavored syrup
- 1/2 cup of milk
- 1 pinch of ground cinnamon

Directions:

- In a mug, mix coconut syrup with espresso. Pour the milk into your saucepan, then heat it at medium to low heat for around 5 minutes until it boils.
- In the espresso mixture, stir the warm milk in. Finish off by sprinkling cinnamon into the latte.

62. Choco Keto Coffee Milkshake

Serving Size: 2

Preparation Time: 5 minutes

Ingredients:

- 2 teaspoons of espresso powder
- 4 teaspoons of cocoa
- 4 ounces of almond milk, unsweetened
- 1 tablespoon of avocado oil
- 2 tablespoons of erythritol sweetener
- 3 ounces of coconut milk, unsweetened
- ¾ cup of water
- 1 ½ cups of ice cubes

Directions:

- In a blender, add espresso powder, cocoa, almond milk, erythritol sweetener, coconut milk and ice cubes.
- Blend until all the ingredients are mixed through, gradually add water until desired consistency is achieved.
- Once ready, transfer to the serving glasses and serve.

63. Hong Kong Style Milk Coffee Tea

Serving Size: 2

Preparation Time: 10 minutes

Ingredients:

- 1 cup of coffee drip
- 1 cup of Hong-Kong style milk tea
- 1/2 – 1 cup of ice cubes

Directions:

- Mix the tea plus coffee in your medium pitcher.
- Add the ice into your 2 glasses, pour tea coffee mix, serve and enjoy!

64. Caramel and Apple Espresso

Serving Size: 1

Preparation Time: 10 minutes

Ingredients:

- 1 cup of apple juice
- 1 tablespoon of caramel sauce (for serving)
- 1 tablespoon of powdered sugar
- ½ cup of cold espresso
- ¼ cup of heavy whipping cream
- 3 tablespoons of caramel sauce
- 5 ice cubes
- Cinnamon

Directions:

- Take a serving glass with ice and pour in the hot espresso, caramel sauce and apple juice. Mix.
- Use a mixer to mix the whipped cream and powdered sugar and use the mixture to decorate the glass.
- Complete by adding a pinch of cinnamon and the caramel sauce on top.

65. Caramel Milk Latte

Serving Size: 1

Preparation Time: 5 minutes

Ingredients:

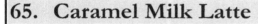

- 2 ounces of espresso
- 10 ounces of milk
- 2 tablespoons of caramel sauce + more for drizzling
- 1 tablespoon of sugar (optional)

Directions:

- Pour the espresso into your mug.
- Pour milk in a saucepan over medium heat, allow to heat for 5 minutes until just starts to boil.
- Then add sugar and caramel sauce to the sauce pan and whisk until blended.
- Make froth using a frother for 25 to 30 seconds.
- Spin your glass, gently tap on the counter until large bubbles appear.
- Hold back foam using the back of a spoon, and add milk into your espresso. Top the coffee with remaining foam, drizzle caramel sauce and serve.

66. Minty White Mocha Frappe

Serving Size: 2

Preparation Time: 5 minutes

Ingredients:

- 3 shots of espresso
- 1 cup of skim milk
- 4 tablespoons of sugar free white chocolate syrup
- 2 tablespoons of sugar free peppermint syrup
- 10-12 cubes of ice
- Whipped cream to serve
- Cubed chocolate wafer bars to serve

Directions:

- In a high-speed blender, add skim milk, espresso, peppermint syrup, white chocolate syrup, and ice cubes. Blend until consistent and smooth.
- Once ready, transfer to 2 chilled glasses. Top with some whipped cream, garnish with cubed chocolate wafer bars and serve.

67. Almond Milk Choco Latte

Serving Size: 1

Preparation Time: 5 minutes

Ingredients:

- 2 shots of brewed espresso
- 1/2 tablespoon of chocolate-hazelnut spread
- 1/2 cup of skim milk
- 1/4 cup of almond milk creamer
- ice cubes, as needed

Directions:

- Mix the chocolate-hazelnut spread and hot espresso in your cup, mix well until melted. Cover and refrigerate for 30 minutes.
- Then add the almond milk creamer, ice and skim milk, mix thoroughly and serve.

68. Red Eye Coffee Espresso

Serving Size: 1

Preparation Time: 15 minutes

Ingredients:

- 1 espresso shot
- 2/3 cup of regular brewed coffee

Directions:

- Take a single shot of espresso. Take brewed coffee in a demitasse cup.
- Pour the shot of espresso in it, and serve!

69. Soy Milk Coffee Crumble Frappe

Serving Size: 2

Preparation Time: 5 minutes

Ingredients:

- 1 cup of soy milk, unsweetened
- 1 cup of strong brewed coffee
- 1/4 cup of cashew nuts
- 1/4 cup of cacao nibs
- 2 tablespoons of sugar-free syrup
- 10 ice cubes

Directions:

- In a blender, add brewed coffee, soy milk, cacao nibs, cashew nuts, sugar-free syrup, and ice.
- Blend the mixture until desired consistency is achieved.
- Once ready, divide the mixture into 2 chilled tall glasses. Add some cacao nibs on top and serve.

70. Lavender Coffee Milk Latte

Serving Size: 1

Preparation Time: 5 minutes

Ingredients:

- 2 ounces of espresso
- 10 ounces milk
- 1 teaspoon of culinary grade lavender buds
- 1 teaspoon of honey, plus more as needed

Directions:

- Transfer the espresso into a mug.
- In a saucepan over moderate heat, add honey, milk and lavender. Heat for 4 to 5 minutes until start to simmer.
- Remove from heat and strain into a glass jar. Remove the lavender buds and discard.
- Make froth using a frother for around 30 seconds.
- Spin your glass, gently tap on the counter until large bubbles appear.
- Hold back foam using the back of a spoon, and add milk into your espresso. Top the coffee with remaining foam, and serve.

71. Continental Coffee Cooler

Serving Size: 1

Preparation Time: 15 minutes

Ingredients:

- 1-1/2 cups of freshly brewed, French roast coffee
- ½ teaspoon of Angostura bitters
- ½ teasopon of pure vanilla extract
- 1-1/2 tablespoon of sugar
- 1 cup of cold club soda
- 4 orange sections

Directions:

- Mix the coffee, vanilla, bitters, plus sugar, and pour into 4 (10-ounce) glasses.
- Fill the glass with ice cubes. Add club soda on top and garnish with orange section.

72. Breakfast Coffee Milk

Serving Size: 6

Preparation Time: 10 minutes

Ingredients:

- 4 cups of whole milk
- 1 & 1/3 cups of strong brewed coffee
- 1/2 cup of maple syrup
- 2 tablespoons of pure molasses
- 2 teaspoons of baking cocoa

For the Whipped Cream:

- 1 cup of heavy whipping cream
- 1 tablespoon of maple syrup
- 1 tablespoon of pure vanilla extract
- Extra baking cocoa

Directions:

- In a saucepan over medium heat, add milk, coffee, maple syrup, molasses and baking cocoa. Stir occasionally and bring the mixture to barely simmering, remove from heat.
- In a small bowl, add cream and beat until it begins to thick. Add vanilla and maple syrup, continue beating until it starts making soft peaks.
- Once ready, transfer the coffee milk to the serving glass. Serve with whipped cream and dust with extra cocoa on top.

73. Café De Olla

Serving Size: 2

Preparation Time: 5 minutes

Ingredients:

- 2 cups of water
- ¼ cup of Mexican coffee, coarsely ground
- 1 large stick of cinnamon
- 1 tablespoon of brown sugar

Directions:

- Pour water in a saucepan over medium heat, add cinnamon, coffee, plus brown sugar and bring the mixture to boil. Then decrease heat and allow the mixture to simmer for 3 to 5 minutes.
- Once ready, strain and pour into coffee mugs, serve immediately.

74. Espresso Hazelnut Balls

Serving Size: 3

Preparation Time: 15 minutes

Ingredients:

- 1 package (9 ounces) of chocolate wafers
- 1 cup of hazelnuts, skinned and toasted
- 1 tablespoon of espresso
- 1 ½ cups of powdered sugar
- 2 ½ tablespoons of light corn syrup
- ½ cup of orange liqueur
- ½ cup of sugar

Directions:

- In a food processor, crush hazelnuts plus wafers, then add the powdered sugar and mix thoroughly, remove and set aside.
- In the same food processor, add espresso, orange liqueur, corn syrup and wafer crumbs, blend until mixture becomes pasty.
- Divide the mixture into equal portions and transform them into ball shape, set aside.
- Add sugar in a separate bowl. Dredge the balls in the sugar and roll to coat evenly. Arrange in the baking sheet lined with parchment paper and place in the refrigerator to age, then serve.

75. Coffee Brownies

Serving Size: 6

Preparation Time: 15 minutes

Cooking Time: 30 minutes

Ingredients:

- 1 cup of all-purpose flour
- 1 pinch of baking powder
- 2 ½ tablespoons of coffee granules
- 3 eggs
- Salt to taste
- 2 ounces of butter
- 1-ounces of chocolate
- 1 teaspoon of vanilla
- 3 tablespoons of sugar
- ¾ cup of mashed walnuts

Directions:

- Prepare the oven and preheat to 380 F.
- In a bowl, mix baking powder, flour, coffee plus salt. In another oven-safe bowl, add butter and chocolate, transfer to the oven and heat until melts.
- Add sugar and eggs to the melted mixture and stir well until fluffy. Then add walnuts and vanilla. Combine both mixtures in a greased saucepan.
- Bake for 20 to 30 minutes. Then remove from heat, allow to cool and cut into equal sized squares using a sharp knife, serve immediately.

76. Chunky Mocha Cookies

Serving Size: 34 cookies

Preparation Time: 15 minutes

Cooking Time: 12 minutes

Ingredients:

- ¾ cup of granulated sugar
- 1 cup of shortening
- 2 eggs
- ½ cup of brown sugar
- 1 tablespoon of coffee granules
- 2 tablespoons of milk
- 2 1/3 cups of plain flour
- 1 teaspoon of vanilla extract
- 1 teaspoon of baking soda
- 2 tablespoons of cocoa powder
- 1 cup of pecans, chopped
- ½ teaspoon of salt
- ¾ cup of raisins
- 1 cup of semisweet chocolate chips
- ¾ cup of flaked coconut

Directions:

- Prepare the oven and preheat to 375 F.
- In a large bowl, add both sugars and shortening, beat until fluffy.
- Then add milk, eggs, vanilla and coffee granules, combine thoroughly.
- Sift cocoa, flour, salt and baking soda in a large bowl.
- Then add raisins, pecans and chocolate chips, combine thoroughly.
- Line tray with parchment paper, place 2 scoops of cookie batter onto the baking tray, and make sure each cookie is 2" apart.
- Transfer the tray to the preheated oven and bake for 10 to 12 minutes until golden brown. Once done, remove from oven, let it cool for 5 to 10 minutes, and then serve.

CHAPTER 8:
Stencil Templates for Your Coffee

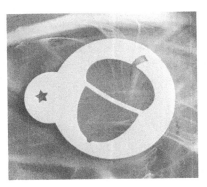
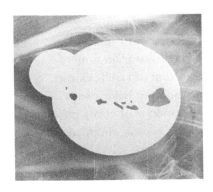

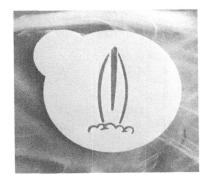

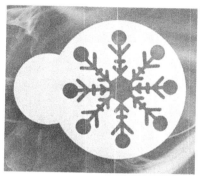

CONCLUSION

Now, you know quite a handful of coffee recipes. If you tried all of them, feel free to go around calling yourself an expert caffeine drinker.

As you may have seen going through the recipes, making coffee is as easy.

The aforementioned ingredients might be blended and combined, and you could add your own secret ingredients to make your own special coffee. If you want, you may even give it your name. Almost nothing could possibly go wrong while preparing coffee.

Knowing these recipes also gives you the advantage of being able to make a flawless cup of coffee by simply substituting your preferred vegan sweetener for any dairy- or non-vegan-based sweetener. Despite being so straightforward, this cookbook is quite useful for brewing a variety of coffees.

There are no precise, rigid guidelines for making coffee. Fortunately, all you need to make these coffees are common household materials and utensils. Making coffee is wonderful because you can experiment with it as much as you like without truly failing. You'll always have a nice beverage in your hand.

You've never had a stronger cup of coffee, or enjoyed a better cappuccino, than when you use the following tippling tips. If you actually love coffee and want to make it your ultimate drink of choice, here are the best ways to make your favorite beverage that much better.

1. Choose the best coffee beans for your tastes. There are many different types of beans to choose from depending on what sort of experience you want out of your cup o' joe. Fair trade beans, conventional arabica beans, or even decaf beans can be found at specialty roasters around the world.
2. Grind it right before brewing it up in order to maximize flavor and aroma superiority.
3. Aim for a bold cup, with rich, intense flavor. For something more on the mild side, you can also opt for an Italian or French roast.
4. Always use whole milk, not low-fat or skim milk. This helps give your coffee a much richer taste.
5. Fill your cup to the max with rich cream, no matter what type of coffee you're drinking. You can choose several different types of cream depending on what sort of experience you want out of your drink. A tawny cow's milk adds a nutty

sweetness to any type of coffee drink; a good quality whole milk adds richness; and half-and-half is the ideal mix for anything lighter in flavor..

6. If you like cream, try using a dollop of vanilla ice cream; this will surely add a kick to the cup.

7. If you like sugar, there are several different types of sugar cubes that you can use in your coffee. Brown sugar adds a caramel-y taste to your coffee; raw sugar adds an interesting flavor to any drink; and even lavender sugar can add a sweet floral taste to your drink.

8. Add some honey for an interesting taste. The flavor of the honey will add more depth and dimension to the drink.

9. Always use fresh spices instead of pre-ground spices when brewing up your morning joe. Adding a dash of cinnamon, nutmeg and ginger can bring a whole new flavor to your coffee.

10. Take time to enjoy your cup of joe. Sip it slowly and savor every last drop.

Another bonus of knowing these recipes is that you could easily replace the dairy or non-vegan sweeteners with the vegan alternatives of your choice and have yourself a perfect coffee. This cookbook is that simple but comes in very handy for making many different coffees.

Making coffee has no particular strict rules. Fortunately, all you use are simple kitchen ingredients and basic kitchen utensils to prepare these coffees. The beauty of making coffee is that you can experiment with them as much as you like and never really go wrong. You will actually always end up with a tasty drink in your hand.

Made in United States
North Haven, CT
11 October 2023

42612225R00057